STUDY GUIDE

to accompany

Edgar/Jewsbury/Hackett/Molony/Gordan

CIVILIZATIONS

Past and Present

Volume One

Twelfth Edition

Norman Love
El Paso Community College

PEARSON

Longman

New York Boston San Francisco
London Toronto Sydney Tokyo Singapore Madrid
Mexico City Munich Paris Cape Town Hong Kong Montreal

Study Guide to accompany Edgar/Jewsbury/Hackett/Molony/Gordan, *Civilizations Past and Present, Volume One, Twelfth Edition*

Copyright ©2008 Pearson Education, Inc.

ISBN: 0-205-58896-4

1 2 3 4 5 6 7 8 9 10–OPM–10 09 08 07

I would like to thank Ms. Dianne Hall
for all of her efficient and gracious assistance.

CONTENTS

TO THE STUDENT

The main purpose of this study guide is to help you get the most out of the text, *Civilization Past & Present*, twelfth edition. In the hands of a conscientious student, this study guide can be a valuable tool. Here are some tips on how to use it effectively.

The organization is easy to grasp. Each chapter in the study guide bears the same number and title as a chapter in the text. Before and after you read a chapter in *Civilization Past & Present*, look at the corresponding study guide chapter. Each study guide chapter begins with a brief overview, followed by a section entitled "You Should Have a Basic Understanding Of." Under this heading is a list of important chapter themes and concepts. It will quickly alert you to the concepts to watch for and learn from each chapter.

The next part of each study guide chapter asks, "Have You Mastered the Basic Facts?" After reading a chapter, try to fill in the blanks with correct identifications. Some of the questions in this section are quite challenging. Do not let mistakes discourage you. Simply try to determine why you missed a particular item. When you check the answer key at the end of each volume, you will probably recognize a few names that you could not recall. If so, you are not mastering the information as you read and a review will probably help your score. If the answer key does not jog your memory, the situation is more serious. Try to find the passage in the text that contains the relevant information. Did you miss a name that the authors stressed? Was an important concept overlooked? Whatever the problem, try to remedy it when you read the next chapter.

Develop a method of study that works for you. Try underlining important facts, terms, and interpretations, but be selective. If you underline too much, reviewing will be difficult. Another simple procedure is to pause briefly after you read a few pages of the text and recite some of the key facts and main points.

When filling in the blanks in this section, make a special effort to spell the names and terms correctly. Spelling mistakes often make an unfavorable impression. Get in the habit of mastering the necessary details and being accurate. The answer key will serve as a handy reference to check your work.

The section "Try These Multiple-Choice Questions" will not only help you review the text, but it will also give you experience in coping with multiple-choice tests. Try to develop the knack for taking this type of examination. Cultivate the habit of reading each question very carefully. Often a single word is of key importance. Answer the easy questions first and then go back to the difficult ones. Before trying to guess an answer, eliminate the choices that seem wrong. If you narrow the range of choice, you improve the odds of hitting the right answer. Usually you should stick with your first guess.

Even if the answer key confirms your guess, you should try to figure out *why* it is the correct answer. Your mistakes should receive even more attention. Did you misread the question? Did you misunderstand a passage in the text? Learning why you made a mistake is more important than finding out the right answer to an examination question.

The middle sections of the study guide chapters vary. Some chapters have a section entitled "The Place," which contains maps and map exercises. These exercises are valuable even if your instructor does not include map questions on examinations. History should not be studied apart from the geographic stage on which events occur.

Time is as important as place, and many of the study guide chapters contain a section called "Relationships in Time." Some people have the mistaken notion that studying history consists primarily of memorizing dates. Historians study and interpret what is significant in the past. Lists of isolated unrelated dates are not very useful in this endeavor. The historical significance of people and events depends on their relationship to other important phenomena. It is more meaningful to know that Copernicus lived and worked before Galileo than to know that the latter was born in the year 1564.

This does not mean that you should never bother remembering dates. Certain key dates can serve as anchors to which you can tie related events. For example, in English history, the Glorious Revolution of 1688 marks a crucial phase in the evolution of constitutional monarchy. Memorizing 1688 as a point of reference will help you remember the historical relationships between James II, William and Mary, the Bill of Rights, and John Locke's influential political philosophy challenging royal absolutism. Other key dates, such as the year the French Revolution broke out or the year World War II ended, serve similar purposes.

If you have trouble remembering chronological relationships and key dates, review them in the study guide several times. You can do this rather quickly. Not all of your studying has to be done in blocks of concentrated work. When you have a few minutes to spare, pick up the study guide and glance at the "Relationships in Time" sections that you have completed. Repeated study should help you recall dates more easily.

In addition to chronological relationships, the study guide stresses connections among a wide variety of people, events, ways of doing things, and ideas. The section "Making Connections" found in some chapters is designed to point out relationships. Historical phenomena are not only more meaningful if they are seen in relation to other developments, but they are also easier to remember.

"Focusing on Major Topics" also encourages you to perceive the text material in meaningful units. Such topics as the contrasting characteristics between ancient Sparta and Athens can be quickly reviewed in these exercises. These sections also help you bring together information that appeared in different parts of a chapter.

The skills you cultivate by studying history are applicable to many fields far removed from college history classes. Reading with comprehension, assimilating information and remembering it, seeing relationships, and drawing conclusions based on evidence are all part of being a history student. These intellectual skills, in addition to the intrinsic value of learning about the past, help explain why history is traditionally part of a good general education. These skills are useful in business, law, politics, and education as well as in the study of history.

The section of the study guide entitled "Do You Know the Significance of These Terms?" clearly reflects the liberal arts value of studying history. It asks you to define words that may be unfamiliar. Some of the words are technical, but many are useful for general discussions. Cultivate the habit of using a dictionary, and try to use the new words whenever you have a suitable opportunity.

All chapters in the study guide have a series of brief quotations expressing the views of eminent thinkers and scholars on topics covered in the text. This section, which is called "Arriving at Conclusions," also contains questions that require you to use information drawn from the text in a manner that is pertinent to the quotation. Some of these questions are similar to those found on many essay examinations.

Try writing out essay answers to some of these questions within fifteen to thirty minutes. The practice will be valuable if you adhere to the fundamentals of writing good essays. Read the quotation carefully and make sure you answer all parts of the question. You may find it helpful to jot down a brief outline before you start writing, but do not waste time. Avoid rambling introductory and concluding paragraphs. Answer precisely the questions asked. Be explicit, and include some detailed information to support your generalizations. Try to write clearly, spell correctly, and follow the rules of good grammar and punctuation. Save enough time to proofread your answer so that you can correct the little mistakes that are common in first drafts of essays

At the end of each chapter you will find additional "Questions to Think About." Some of these are similar to questions on essay examinations, but they are designed primarily to stimulate thought and to introduce important issues. History can be endlessly fascinating. It provides an inexhaustible font of human experience, which can help you become intellectually more sophisticated and mature. Using this study guide to study *Civilization Past & Present* can yield rewards that are far more important than good grades, although we hope you will earn high marks as well.

TO THE INSTRUCTOR

This study guide is designed to help students review the narrative of history as found in the corresponding chapters of *Civilization Past & Present* and to add depth and breadth to their understanding of history and its processes. It has been prepared for use with the twelfth edition of the text.

An introduction addressed to the student not only describes the study guide but provides tips on how to use it most effectively. It includes advice on how to answer objective and essay examination questions as well as some comments on the value of studying history.

Each chapter of *the* study guide begins with a brief chapter overview and a list of the major concepts dealt with in the corresponding chapter of *Civilization Past & Present*. It succinctly gives the student an idea of what he or she should watch for and learn.

The overview and list of major concepts are followed by two standard sections, fill-in-the-blank identifications and multiple-choice questions. These test items will help the student review the basic facts in each chapter.

In the feature called "The Place," the study guide adheres to the philosophy that history cannot be studied apart from the geographic stage on which events occur. Thus, maps and map exercises appear in most of the chapters.

The exercises entitled "Relationships in Time" emphasize putting items in chronological order and perceiving relationships. This approach is explained in the introduction addressed to the student. The student is asked to remember only a small number of key dates, which can serve as useful points of reference.

Many chapters contain another feature entitled "Focusing on Major Topics," which provides various exercises designed to help the student gain a clearer, more detailed understanding of particular subjects. The exercises under the heading "Making Connections" also provide additional review, although they are designed primarily to help the student see relationships.

The introduction addressed to the student points out that the study of history promotes the development of important skills that are an essential part of any good general education, reading with comprehension, assimilating information and remembering it, seeing relationships, and drawing conclusions based on evidence. The liberal arts value of the study guide is further enhanced by a feature that promotes the development of a better vocabulary. It simply asks the student to define words that may be unfamiliar. Some of the terms are technical, but many of the words are generally useful.

"Arriving at Conclusions" is a section containing brief quotations expressing the views of noted scholars. The questions accompanying each quotation require the student to draw information from the text and apply it in ways that are pertinent to the quotation.

Each chapter of the study guide ends with a list of additional questions designed to stimulate thought and raise issues. Many of these "Questions to Think About" are well-suited for classroom discussion.

The study guide attempts to reach all levels of student abilities. Questions and exercises range from the fundamental to the sophisticated, from the traditional to the unexpected. An effort has also been made to relate the knowledge and wisdom acquired from a study of the past to the problems and complexities of today's world. Whether used as a tool by the individual student, or as a general classroom supplement, it offers both a valuable study aid and an intellectual challenge.

CHAPTER 1

Stone Age Societies and the Earliest Civilizations of the Near East

For most of human history, human beings struggled against the forces of Nature and their own limitations, eking out an existence based on primitive living conditions. Gradually, with the passage of thousands of years, during which they lived their lives as hunters and gatherers, people turned to settlement along major rivers, began to grow staple crops, used technology to meet their needs, and increasingly worked together in groups for common purposes. In the process, they created civilizations.

By the fourth millennium B.C.E. in the Near East, ancient peoples were well on their way to becoming societies with distinct economic, political, social, and cultural characteristics, having their own particular interests and value systems. In the area that became known as the Fertile Crescent, the focus of this chapter, we will see how these early cultures, remarkably diverse yet assimilating and influencing each other, laid the framework for what we know as civilization today.

YOU SHOULD HAVE A BASIC UNDERSTANDING OF:

The stages of early human technological progress and cultural development.

The significance of the transition from food-gathering to food-producing economies.

Preliterate cultures.

Preliterate society and religion.

Why and how civilization took root in Mesopotamia.

Egypt's culture along the Nile.

Mesopotamian successors to Babylon.

The Persians.

HAVE YOU MASTERED THE BASIC FACTS?

Fill in each of the following blanks with the correct identification.

The Development of Humankind

1. _____: "Prehumans" or "protohumans."

2. _____: The first tool-maker.

3. _____: Emerged in Africa as long as 2.3 million years ago, walked upright, and learned to use and control fire; also known as *Homo ergaster*.

4. _____: Hypothetical "mother" of human beings whose DNA sample dates to approximately 200,000 years ago in Eastern Africa.

Preliterate Cultures

5. _____: "Dawn stones"—pieces of stone used to perform an immediate task; their use led to tool-making.

6. _____: Age in which use of stone implements was the most distinctive feature.

7. _____: Prehistoric cultural stage characterized by the domestication of plants and animals and the establishment of settled farming communities.

8. _____: Region of arable soil with adequate rainfall or water available for irrigation, stretching from the Mediterranean Sea to the Persian Gulf and including the world's earliest civilizations.

9. _____: Village in southern Turkey dating to around 6500 to 5400 B.C.E.; best example of a Neolithic village found to date.

Preliterate Society and Religion

10. _____: A revered animal or natural object often used by preliterate clans as a symbol of identity.

11. _____: Megalithic complex in England dating to around 1500 B.C.E.

12. _____: Fertility deity portrayed as a carved female figure with exaggerated sexual features.

Mesopotamia

13. _____: Form of writing developed by the Sumerians.

14. _____: Babylonian epic expressing hope of everlasting life.

15. _____: Akkadian ruler of the third millennium B.C.E. whose empire extended from the Persian Gulf to the Mediterranean Sea.

16. _____: Most outstanding king of the Old Babylonian Empire, best known for compilation of nearly 300 laws.

Egypt

17. _____: Title given to Egyptian rulers assumed to be gods by Egyptians and in whose hands political authority was centralized during the period of the Old Kingdom.

18. _____: Belief in the existence of only one god, embraced briefly by the Egyptian Akhenaton and enduringly by the Hebrews.

19. _____: Early form of Egyptian pictorial writing.

20. _____: Monumental tombs built by Old Kingdom Egyptians to house mummified rulers.

21. _____: Egyptian queen who ruled Egypt during the New Kingdom era, sponsored building programs, and promoted trade.

22. _____: Egypt's most popular religious cult was devoted to him, the fertility god of the Nile, whose death and resurrection were thought to sustain life in Egypt.

Mesopotamian Successors to Babylon

23. _____: People famous for their early skill in working iron.

24. _____: Important trading people of the ancient world, primarily responsible for the development of alphabetic writing.

25. _____: Tenth-century B.C.E. ruler of the Hebrews whose name became synonymous with wisdom.

26. _____: The history of the Hebrews, as recorded in the Old Testament, begins with this patriarchal clan leader who led his people out of Ur into Canaan around 1800 B.C.E.

27. _____: Their army, with chariots, mounted cavalry, and sophisticated siege engines, was the most powerful in the ancient world before 700 B.C.E.

28. _____: Chaldean ruler who made Babylon the most impressive city of the day, with its Hanging Gardens and the temple known in the Bible as the "Tower of Babel."

The Persians

29. _____: The Persian ruler considered the greatest conqueror in the history of the Near East.

30. _____: The 1600-mile road between Sardis and Susa that tied together the heart of the Persian Empire with the Mediterranean Sea.

31. _____: The official religion of the Persian Empire emphasizing justice, righteous thoughts, and actions.

TRY THESE MULTIPLE-CHOICE QUESTIONS

1. _____ The skeletons of which of the following would be virtually indistinguishable from humans today? (1) *Australopithecus africanus*; (2) Cro-Magnon; (3) Neanderthal; (4) *Homo ergaster*; (5) *Homo habilis*.

2. _____ Most primitive cultures include (1) some system of justice; (2) a government with some democratic traits; (3) a strong religious influence; (4) artistic expression; (5) all of the above.

3. _____ The technological developments of *Homo sapien* culture during the late Paleolithic phase included (1) the creation of tools that were used to make other tools; (2) the first human-made buildings; (3) the bow; (4) division of labor; (5) all of the above.

4. _____ Late-Paleolithic peoples' reverence for the spirits of the animals they hunted and the fertility of humans was expressed by (1) burial mounds to preserve animal remains; (2) temples dedicated to certain animals; (3) the Earth Mother goddess; (4) domesticating large animals, keeping them as pets; (5) painting scenes from the hunt.

3

5. _____ In preliterate societies, the concept of justice is most concerned with (1) punishment of offenders; (2) protecting the rights of individuals; (3) promoting equality; (4) maintaining order or equilibrium; (5) protecting the property of individuals.

6. _____ Which of the following terms most accurately describes governing political bodies in food-gathering cultures? (1) egalitarian; (2) aristocratic; (3) animistic; (4) monarchical; (5) none of the above.

7. _____ The order in which most ancient cultures learned to use various kinds of metals was probably (1) iron, bronze, copper; (2) bronze, copper, iron; (3) copper, bronze, iron; (4) iron, copper, bronze; (5) copper, iron, bronze.

8. _____ Which of the following lay outside the Fertile Crescent? (1) Memphis; (2) Ur; (3) Tyre; (4) Babylon; (5) Jerusalem.

9. _____ Cuneiform writing gets its name from (1) the priesthood that had a monopoly of its use; (2) the use of phonics; (3) a kind of stylus used by the scribes; (4) the clay tablets that were a common writing medium; (5) the shape of the impressions made.

10. _____ Civilization is usually defined as including (1) a written language; (2) urban living; (3) division of labor; (4) permanent architecture; (5) all of the above.

11. _____ The first true emperor in history: (1) Ashurburnipal; (2) Menes; (3) Sargon I; (4) Ramses II; (5) Nebuchadnezzer.

12. _____ Most of the great pyramids in Egypt were built during the (1) Predynastic period; (2) Intermediate Kingdom; (3) Old Kingdom; (4) Middle Kingdom; (5) New Kingdom.

13. _____ Egyptian religion and architecture both suggest an overwhelming preoccupation with (1) social reform; (2) technological advance and economic change; (3) monotheism; (4) the Nile; (5) all of the above.

14. _____ The use of war and conquest as a central part of economic life was characteristic of the (1) Aramaeans; (2) Assyrians; (2) Hebrews; (3) Egyptians; (4) Sumerians.

15. _____ Choose the correct chronological sequence for empire building in the Near East: (1) Persian, Assyrian, Hittite, Chaldean; (2) Chaldean, Assyrian, Hittite, Persian; (3) Hittite, Assyrian, Chaldean, Persian; (4) Assyrian, Persian, Hittite, Chaldean.

16. _____ The Egyptian Book of the Dead (1) described the short, tragic reign of King Tutankhamen; (2) was often placed in the tombs of the deceased to help them in the afterlife; (3) told the story of Isis and Osiris; (4) was the sacred scripture of the early Zoroastrians; (5) none of the above.

17. _____ The Hebrews' most significant contribution to history was in the area of (1) mathematics and science; (2) astrology and astronomy; (3) political theory; (4) religion and ethics; (5) painting and sculpture.

18. _____ The Hebrew Exodus from Egypt under Moses occurred during the reign of Pharaoh (1) Menkaure; (2) Ramses II; (3) Amenhotep III; (4) Necho II; (5) Thutmose III.

19. _____ In ancient Mesopotamia, the institution of slavery was based primarily on (1) military obligation; (2) conquest and debt; (3) racial characteristics; (4) cultural differences; (5) religious beliefs.

20. _____ The most significant achievement of King Hammurabi of Babylon was (1) Babylon's conquest of Egypt; (2) the first use of horse-drawn chariots in warfare; (3) creating the Hanging Gardens; (4) his code of law; (5) his military exploits.

21. _____ Because of the unpredictability of the rivers in Mesopotamia, the people there in ancient times: (1) refused to cooperate with each other; (2) lived in constant awe of their gods for fear they might bring destruction on them; (3) never developed stable societies; (4) looked to the afterlife as a time of peace and fulfillment; (5) regularly sought to make military alliances with other settlements.

22. _____ The prophet in early sixth-century Persia who developed a religion centered on the sole god, Ahura-Mazda: (1) Darius; (2) Osiris; (3) Ashburnipal; (4) Zoroaster; (5) Isis.

RELATIONSHIPS IN TIME

Please place the following items under the correct column below.

use of eoliths
cultivation of grains
domestication of animals
use of polished stone tools

standardization of tools
invention of the bow
semi-sedentary lifestyle
adopted
first man-made building

Çatal Hüyük
Stonehenge was built
shift toward food production
pyramids of Giza

Paleolithic   **Neolithic**

THE PLACE

On the following map, write the name of each item listed in the appropriate place. Use the maps in Chapter 1 of your textbook as sources of information.

A. **Regions**   B. **Rivers**   C. **Seas/Gulfs**   D. **Cities**

Sumer   Euphrates   Persian   Babylon
Arabia   Nile   Gulf   Memphis
Egypt   Tigris   Black Sea   Thebes
Media   Adriatic   Nineveh
Persia   Sea   Jerusalem
Mesopotamia   Red Sea
          Mediterranean
          Sea

E.   *Shade in the Fertile Crescent like this: ////////.*

DO YOU KNOW THE SIGNIFICANCE OF THESE TERMS?

In Chapter 1, these terms represent important events and tendencies in world history. In the space provided, identify each of the following and evaluate its historical significance.

Homo sapiens

tribe

Çatal Hüyük

Earth Mother (Mother Goddess)

lugal

megaliths

Epic of Gilgamesh

Hammurabi's Code

Nile River

biblia

Ramses II

Pyramids of Kush

Yahweh

Aramaic

Zoroastrianism

ARRIVING AT CONCLUSIONS

Here are some quotations from eminent scholars dealing with aspects of this period of history. Answer the accompanying questions and be prepared to defend your position.

1. "Why did he come to caves like this, live in them, and then make paintings of animals not where he lived but in places that were dark, secret, remote, hidden, inaccessible? In these places the animal was [obviously] magical. We still want to know [however] what power the hunters believed they got from the paintings. I think that [it] . . . is the power of anticipation: the forward-looking imagination. The hunter was made familiar with dangers which he knew he had to face but to which he had not yet come. When the hunter was brought here into the secret dark and the light was suddenly flashed on the pictures, he saw the bison as he would have to face him. . . . The moment of fear was made present to him; his spear-arm flexed with an experience which he would have and which he needed not to be afraid of." (Jacob Bronowski, *The Ascent of Man* [Boston: Little, Brown, 1973], p. 54.)

From what you have learned about Cro-Magnon man, do you agree or disagree with Bronowski's interpretation? Why? Can similar use of magic, as Bronowski defines it, be found in modern civilization?

2. "The fourteenth and thirteenth centuries [B.C.E.] witnessed an exchange of people, goods, and ideas between the countries bordering the east Mediterranean basin on a scale unprecedented in Levantine prehistory. This . . . was no revolution, as the foundations had been well-laid in the sixteenth and fifteenth centuries [B.C.E.], but . . . a phenomenon of the age and led to the highest degree of material affluence and cultural cross-fertilization achieved during the bronze age. Nor did these interactions betoken a lessening of belligerency or warfare . . . between the pharaohs of Egypt, the Hittite emperors, and the Mitannian kings. This constant state of armed confrontation, which did not interfere with trade, culminated in the mass movement of peoples at the end of the thirteenth century [B.C.E.]." (Robert S. Merrillees, "Political Conditions in the Eastern Mediterranean During the Bronze Age," *Biblical Archaeologist*, March 1986, p. 50.)

When was the Bronze Age? What were its most important technological advances? What exchange of ideas took place then? What relationship can you discern between warfare and economic or cultural progress?

QUESTIONS TO THINK ABOUT

1. Explain what is culture and what is civilization. How are they related?

2. What intellectual and physical qualities make humans unique? What are the similarities and differences between modern humans and their prehistoric ancestors?

3. What were distinguishing economic, social, political, and cultural characteristics of humans in the Paleolithic era?

4. Why did early humans develop tools? What motivated them to improve their tool-making skills over time? How did technology change their lives?

5. What impact did the transition from food-gathering to food-producing economies have on human society and culture?

6. Explain how and why the migration of people in the ancient Near East played such an important role in world history.

7. Evaluate the importance of water to the ancient civilizations discussed in Chapter 1 in terms of its socioeconomic and cultural significance. Specifically, compare and contrast its impact on Mesopotamia and Egypt.

8. How did writing help transform the societies of the Fertile Crescent?

9. Explain how Egyptians' concern with the afterlife affected their political system and their culture. What is it about their civilization that has fascinated people through the ages?

10. Analyze how the Sumerians, Phoenicians, Hebrews, and Persians have had an important impact on people in the twenty-first century.

CHAPTER 2

Early Chinese Civilization: From Neolithic Origins to 220 C.E.

The power of Chinese civilization rests mainly in continuity and accumulation of refinements of institutions begun in the past. Search for order in government, the family, and the society in China has resulted in a nation characterized by dynasties, well-defined roles between young and old, male and female, rich and poor, and clearly defined behavior, based on strong philosophical underpinnings. The people of China have tended to turn within to look for answers to their major questions about these issues, all the time shaping and molding the essence of Chinese strength and integrity. The Chinese struggled to find the right formulae that would assure power and prosperity to what would become the largest population in the world—in ancient times just as today. In achieving a mighty empire by 220 C.E., they provide us with a wonderful example of how philosophies translated into government and social order.

The Confucian philosophy of China addressed the problems of human society so simply and directly that it was applied not only in government and education but also in family matters in households throughout China and later in the Chinese-influenced societies of Korea, Japan, and Indochina. To this day, Confucianism inspires a typically tight-knit family group, which reveres its aged members. Mencius's right of rebellion against evil rulers, Confucius's "Golden Rule," and the common-sense ideal of a government based on virtue were all admired outside China and gave inspiration to the eighteenth-century European Enlightenment philosophers.

Man does not live by morality alone. If China had remained a simple agrarian family-like state, Confucianism in its original form might have sufficed. However, to assure broader and more diverse economic control and adequate military power for an empire, Legalist principles were selectively added to the Chinese governing philosophical orthodoxy. These Legalist elements brought pragmatic realism, practical methods of regulating the population, and a blueprint for a working bureaucratic structure. Elements of Daoism introduced into Confucianism brought mystical and individualistic aspects into Chinese civilization. All these were synthesized in the Han dynasty into a system that offered a single comprehensive answer to the full range of human problems and needs.

YOU SHOULD HAVE A BASIC UNDERSTANDING OF:

The geographic environment that shaped Chinese society.

The common themes that carry over from prehistoric into historic China.

What China was like during the Shang and Zhou dynasties.

The principles of Confucianism, Legalism, and Daoism.

The manifestations of art, technology, and statecraft that emerged under Qin and Han.

The elements that caused a cycle of rise and fall during the Qin and Han dynasties.

China's foreign contacts and attitude toward the outside world.

HAVE YOU MASTERED THE BASIC FACTS?

Fill in each of the following blanks with the correct identification.

Creation of China

1. _____: This river crosses the west and north of China, where millet and wheat became major crops.

2. _____: The second major river, south of which is a fertile valley noted for rice growing, silk, and tea.

3. _____: The name given to the sage rulers thought to have given China its government and technology.

4. _____: Heated bones used to interpret the future, prominent in Neolithic China.

5. _____: The name of the culture in northern China that came to dominate by about 1600 B.C.E.

6. _____ and _____: The twin opposite but complementary forces in the universe.

7. _____: A major religious element that supported Shang rulers.

8. _____: Material used to make drinking vessels, weapons, pottery, and various art objects during the Shang period.

9. _____: Shang queen whose tomb contained incredible riches, art objects, and oracle bones, which testify to her high social status and political power.

10. _____: Term used to describe the period in Chinese history (403–221 B.C.E.) following the collapse of the Zhou dynasty.

Zhou Dynasty

11. _____: This book explained why the Zhou replaced the Shang.

12. _____: This metal provided a breakthrough in agriculture in the Zhou dynasty.

13. _____: Written characters that depict an object or an idea.

Philosophical Schools

14. _____: Confucius's real name.

15. _____: A collection of Confucius's answers to questions asked by his disciples.

16. _____: Chinese term for superior man or gentleman.

17. _____ : He was largely responsible for the emergence of Confucianism as the most widely accepted philosophy in China.

18. _____ : The Chinese idea of a kind of permission to rule based on the ruler's goodness.

19. _____ : Leading philosopher of Daoism.

20. _____ :The Legalist philosophy is most clearly associated with this dynasty.

Qin China

21. _____ : Chief minister of the state of Qin during the Warring States who shaped the Legalist doctrine.

22. _____ : First emperor of China and of the Qin dynasty.

23. _____ : The more than 6,000 figures discovered in the tomb of the First Emperor in 1974; they are among the greatest archaeological finds in history.

Han China

24. _____ : Known as Emperor Gaozu, he founded the Han dynasty in 206 B.C.E.

25. _____ : Called Huns in the West, these nomads threatened the Chinese in the second century B.C.E.

26. _____ : The main Chinese commodity traded to the West.

27. _____ : The name of the most vigorous of the Han emperors; his name is associated with the height of the Han dynasty.

28. _____ : Author of the world's first dictionary, which contained 9,000 characters, their meaning, and pronunciation.

29. _____ : Confucian advisor to Emperor Wudi, he collected stories of 125 heroic women to serve as positive role models for court ladies and the emperor.

30. _____ : Major trade routes connecting China and the West, which continued for more than a millennium after the Han dynasty.

TRY THESE MULTIPLE-CHOICE QUESTIONS

1. _____ The first historic state in China developed in the valley of the following river: (1) Tarim; (2) Yangtze; (3) Yellow; (4) Han; (5) Hsi.

2. _____ The Shang people were adept at (1) pyramid building; (2) contour plowing; (3) figure painting; (4) bronze metallurgy; (5) iron casting.

3. _____ Choose the correct chronological order among the following dynasties: (1) Han, Shang, Qin, Zhou; (2) Zhou, Qin, Han, Shang; (3) Shang, Zhou, Qin; Han; (4) Qin, Han, Shang, Zhou; (5) Qin, Zhou, Shang, Han.

4. _____ This ruler united China and suppressed all philosophies EXCEPT Legalism: (1) Liu Pang; (2) Huangdi; (3) Wudi; (4) Liu Bang; (5) Wu Ding.

5. _____ The Yangshao Neolithic people are noted for their (1) pottery; (2) pictographs; (3) silk; (4) terra-cotta; (5) spears.

6. _____ The following is NOT TRUE of the Shang people: (1) they used the chariot in war; (2) they used an alphabetic writing system; (3) they made human sacrifices; (4) they buried nobility in tombs; (5) they produced *taotie*.

7. _____ The Mandate of Heaven (1) was based on ancestor worship; (2) made rulers into gods; (3) assumed that only virtuous rulers were acceptable to *Tian*; (4) guaranteed popular control of government; (5) was first introduced in the Han dynasty.

8. _____ Confucianism (1) is egalitarian; (2) looks to the gods and spirits for assistance; (3) is very legalistic; (4) centers on human society; (5) is highly individualistic.

9. _____ Mencius believed (1) people are inherently evil; (2) monarchy is necessary for stability; (3) all people are equal; (4) democratic rule is best; (5) people are innately good.

10. _____ Legalists believed in all the following ideas EXCEPT (1) human nature is good; (2) law must be equally applied; (3) education is useless; (4) state loyalty supersedes family loyalty; (5) fixed penalties apply to all.

11. _____ The Qin dynasty (1) was toppled by popular revolt; (2) unified China; (3) was anxious to suppress competing philosophies; (4) engaged in book burning; (5) all of the above.

12. _____ The famous terra-cotta warrior army guards the tomb of (1) the last Han emperor; (2) the first Qin emperor; (3) the first Han emperor; (4) the first Zhou emperor; (5) the first Shang emperor.

13. _____ The Han dynasty succeeded in lasting much longer than Qin because (1) they used, rather than persecuted, Confucian scholars; (2) they succeeded in burning all books; (3) they finally succeeded in building the Great Wall; (4) they had fewer outside enemies; (5) they emphasized military power rather than ethics.

14. _____ Han examinations for government service (1) brought into government many merchants; (2) were highly discriminatory; (3) were theoretically open to all capable men; (4) were open only to aristocrats; (5) encouraged universal education in China.

15. _____ All of the following helped cause a decline in the Han dynasty EXCEPT: (1) increased taxes; (2) large landowners controlling more of the population; (3) tax-free estates decreased in number; (4) coinage was debased; (5) overextension of the empire.

16. _____ Wang Mang (1) was a Qin emperor; (2) succeeded in saving China with his reform program; (3) tried but failed to put through a reform program; (4) was a leader of Daoist rebels; (5) rejected Zhou-style management.

17. _____ Chinese history writing, beginning in the Han dynasty, is characterized by (1) the fixed image of a golden age in the past; (2) incorporation of magic and superstitious practices; (3) the need for constant change of man's institutions; (4) an emphasis on literary quality; (5) writing official histories of the previous dynasty.

18. _____ The Emperor Wudi (1) dramatically expanded China's borders; (2) raised the peasants' taxes; (3) increased military service; (4) started government monopolies; (5) all of the above.

19. _____ In the exchange of goods between Han China and the West, (1) Western goods were highly valued and caused gold and silver outflow from China; (2) Chinese merchants traveled to the West; (3) Chinese adopted the more advanced Western technology; (4) high-value Chinese silk items went west and were in great demand; (5) the balance of trade favored the West.

20. _____ In its present form, the Great Wall of China was mainly the work of (1) the Zhou; (2) the Qin; (3) the Han; (4) all of the above; (5) none of the above.

MAKING CONNECTIONS

Beside each item, place a D for Daoism, an L for Legalism, an M for Mencius, and a C for Confucius, depending on what is appropriate.

1. _____ Author of the *Analects*.

2. _____ His basic concern was for the individual.

3. _____ Taught that the ruler had to be virtuous or lose the Mandate of Heaven.

4. _____ Mencius was his most illustrious disciple.

5. _____ The Golden Rule sums up his main concern.

6. _____ Held that people are basically evil and act virtuously only when compelled to do so.

7. _____ Advocated "non-action."

8. _____ Suggested that people have the right to rebel against and even kill bad rulers.

9. _____ Gave the word "Dao" a metaphysical meaning, linking it with nature.

10. _____ Emphasized a harsh, inflexible law code as a means to orderly society.

11. _____ Revolted against both society and the limits of intellect.

12. _____ Unification of China in 221 B.C.E. was largely the result of practicing this philosophy.

13. _____ The idea that a bad ruler would fall and be replaced by a more capable ruler was taken up by this man.

14. _____ Suggested withdrawing from the chaos and evil of society and pursuing a passive individualism.

15. _____ Insisted that all people are innately good.

16. _____ Drew an analogy between man's tendency to do good and water flowing downward.

17. _____ Drew an analogy between man's incompetence to know what is right.

18. _____ Bases his philosophy on inspiration from the past Golden Age.

19. _____ Instinct and intuition are more important than learning and reasoning.

20. _____ Loyalty to the state supersedes family loyalties.

DO YOU KNOW THE SIGNIFICANCE OF THESE TERMS?

This chapter contains numerous terms that represent important events and tendencies in world history, some of which are listed below. In the space provided below, identify each of the following and evaluate its historical significance.

Shang dynasty

"oracle bones"

Tian

Mandate of Heaven

Yin and *yang*

li

Warring States Period

The Five Sovereigns

Ban Zhao

Mencius

First Emperor

Spring and Autumn Period

Han Era

Historical Records

silk trade

THE PLACE

On the map below, locate and label these places, using the maps in the text chapter.

India	Indian Ocean	Outer Mongolia	Tibet
Yangtze River	Bay of Bengal	Arabian Sea	Yellow Sea
Ch'ang An	Hsi (Si) River	Yellow River	South China Sea
East Indies	China	Korea	Pacific Ocean

A. *Shade in the approximate area of Shang dynasty control.*

B. *With small arrows, indicate the direction of expansion during the Zhou dynasty and the approximate extent of that expansion, based on material in the text.*

C. *With further small arrows, indicate the approximate extent of the Qin dynasty expansion, based on the text.*

D. *With large arrows, indicate the direction and approximate extent of expansion under the Han dynasty, based on material in the text.*

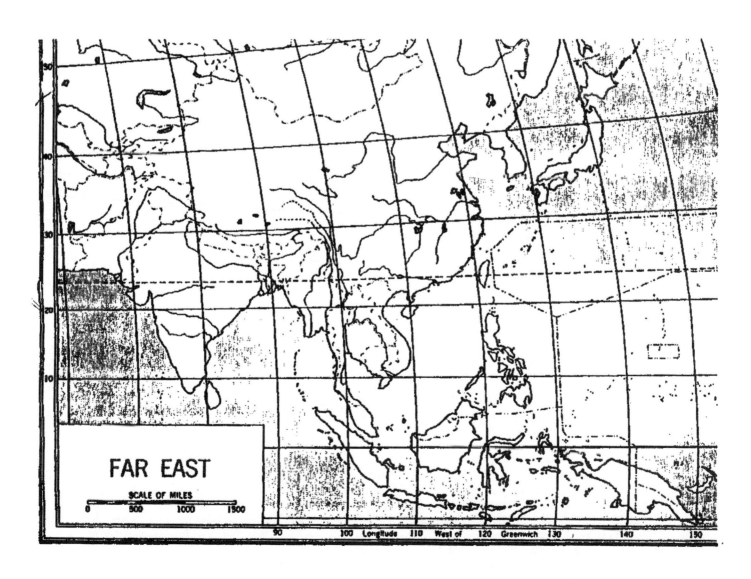

FAR EAST

SCALE OF MILES

0   500   1000   1500

RELATIONSHIPS IN TIME

Events in the earliest river civilizations in China and the Fertile Crescent often ran parallel. Using what you have learned in Chapters 1 and 2, place the items below in the appropriate column and chronological position on the time line below. Alongside the respective lines, bracket and label the time period covered by each of the items listed. (Some of the items will overlap with others, since one of the objectives of time lines is to point out what was going on in various parts of the world in a particular era.)

Qin dynasty
Shang dynasty
Zhou dynasty
Confucius
Han dynasty

Hammurabi
Old Kingdom in Egypt
Persian Empire
Moses
Assyrian Empire

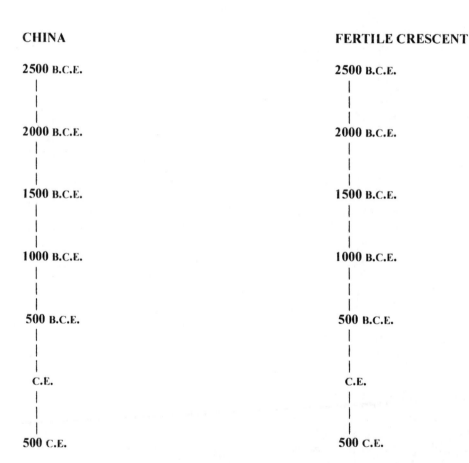

CHINA

2500 B.C.E.

2000 B.C.E.

1500 B.C.E.

1000 B.C.E.

500 B.C.E.

C.E.

500 C.E.

FERTILE CRESCENT

2500 B.C.E.

2000 B.C.E.

1500 B.C.E.

1000 B.C.E.

500 B.C.E.

C.E.

500 C.E.

ARRIVING AT CONCLUSIONS

Here are some quotations from eminent historians dealing with the significance of this period of history. Answer the accompanying questions briefly and be prepared to defend your position.

1. "Since men have likes and dislikes, they can be manipulated by rewards and punishments, the 'two handles' of the ruler's administration. Commands and prohibitions insure the carrying out of the laws, which are nothing more than decrees of the ruler, who has such control of his subjects that he exercises the power of life and death over them. It is the ruler who makes the laws but after they have been promulgated he cannot change them at will. He as well as the people must abide by them in

order that there may be the rule of law. Here the quiescence of the Taoists became a factor. If power is established, the method of rule operating and the laws are in effect, the ruler may practice non-activity . . . the result is that the country is properly governed." (James K. Feibleman, *Understanding Oriental Philosophy* [New York: New American Library, 1976], p. 120.)

Does the above analysis of Legalism call for a perpetual dictatorship under a supreme ruler? Under what circumstances might it be possible for the ruler to relax his life-and-death grip on the people? Do you believe that it is possible to achieve this "withering away of the state" wherein the people become so accustomed to the rules that they can "play the game without an umpire"?

2. "There is a famous story from the Taoist Chuang Tzu: 'Once I dreamt that I was a butterfly, fluttering here and there; in all ways a butterfly. I enjoyed my freedom as a butterfly, not knowing that I was Chuang Tzu. Suddenly I awoke and was surprised to be myself again. Now, how can I tell whether I was a man who dreamt that he was a butterfly, or whether I am a butterfly who dreams that she is a man?'" (Chung-yuan Chang, *Creativity and Taoism: A Study of Chinese Philosophy, Art and Poetry* [New York: Harper and Row, 1963], p. 20.)

Have you ever engaged in an activity in which you "lost yourself," becoming unconscious of time, your surroundings, or other people? Was the experience pleasurable? Did you feel more competent, efficient, or effective? Perhaps you experienced the Tao.

3. "In the opinion of Confucius, models which were supremely worth imitating had to be sought in antiquity. The Master himself lived at a time of social and political instability consequent on the disintegration of the feudal type of society which characterized the early Chou period. . . . Confucius had thought that the solution to China's social and political problems still lay in a revival of early Chou values. . . .
    "Since China was isolated from other major civilizations and unaware of any great cultural tradition apart from its own, it could not seek a solution to its difficulties by borrowing ideas from another society. It did not have experience of alternative systems of government, such as democracy or oligarchy, so that the only obvious means of salvation was a ruler who would govern virtuously in the manner of the Chou founders. . . . Therefore what was of supreme importance in Confucius' eyes was the investigation and transmission of the correct traditions concerning the Golden Age of antiquity. If there was an ideal Way to be rediscovered, transmission of that ideal was what was needed and creativity was unnecessary. . . ." (Raymond Dawson, *Confucius* [New York: Hill and Wang, 1982], pp. 11–12.)

What would Confucius think of the modern notion of progress and our admiration for creativity and innovation? Would acceptance of Confucius's notions hamper China's later attempt to modernize? When later generations of Chinese wanted to modernize, where would they have to go to borrow new ideas?

QUESTIONS TO THINK ABOUT

1. From the study you have made thus far of civilization in the Fertile Crescent and China, would you say that states and their cultures, however brilliant, are destined to decline? Why or why not?

2. Some philosophies can become successful blueprints for government and social structure. What might have been some of the reasons Legalism did not succeed in prolonging the Qin dynasty more than a short fifteen years?

3. How do you account for the fact that art and literature generally flourish during periods of stable government, as in Han China, while philosophy and religion are likely to flourish during periods of change and disorder, as with Confucius and Zuangzi?

4.   The Shang dynasty, as well as the Egyptian and Mesopotamian civilizations, all arose in river valleys. What factors do you think might account for the role of rivers in encouraging early civilizations to emerge?

5.   We tend to see Chinese history as a series of cycles—the rise, fall, and rise of succeeding dynasties with repetitive patterns—and not, as in Western histories, as a progression of improvements through time. Is this because the Han historians set the pattern and we follow them? Is it because there really are repeating elements in the Chinese dynastic state?

6.   What aspects of a civilization are beneficial to its inhabitants? What aspects might be burdensome or exploitive?

7.   In what ways does modern China show the influences of ancient China today? In what ways has China changed?

CHAPTER 3

Early Indian Civilizations: From Neolithic Origins to 300 C.E.

In the modern world, India is not regarded as one of the dominant powers. It faces huge problems of religious division, unstable government, and provision of basic services for a huge and growing population. How do we reconcile this modern condition with the fact that India is one of the areas of the world that rests solidly on a heritage that goes back almost 5,000 years? Does the collective genius that produces governments, philosophies, economies, societies, and religions simply get lost? Or is this genius irrelevant to a modern world? We can speculate about the latter question, but we can be assured that a people does not lose the mental faculties that are capable of producing great ideas. Today, individual Indians excel in all of the areas of modern life and continually remind us that the collective genius that produced Hinduism, Buddhism, the wisdom of the *Arthashastra*, and the stable unity of the Mauryan Empire may not be lost but is only waiting for a modern opportunity to achieve greatness again.

We may also speculate on how the different paths Indians explored in religious discovery may offer some variety insofar as they differ from Western religious traditions. Hinduism, Jainism, and Buddhism all contained an image of the individual as being part of a universal totality. They would be unhappy until worldly ties were broken and unity with all existence is realized. This differs from Western materialism. Likewise, ideas of reincarnation and karmic retribution set India on paths very different from Western and Middle Eastern beliefs in a single guiding deity. The Hindu caste system, for all the criticisms of its divisions, stabilizes Indian society in a way that is hard to give up. Ascetic self-denial is still a respected lifestyle in India. The grandeur of the Vedic period and Mauryan Empire still inspires Indians more than 2,000 years later. It explains their deep sense of pride in spite of economic and political difficulties. India is perhaps poor only in the collective materialistic sense.

YOU SHOULD HAVE A BASIC UNDERSTANDING OF:

The rise of civilization in the Indus Valley.

The culture patterns that were formed during the Vedic Age and are still evident in modern India.

The religions of India.

The Mauryan Empire.

The artistic and literary richness that India has inherited from its past.

The process of give and take with outside peoples who fertilized Indian civilization.

HAVE YOU MASTERED THE BASIC FACTS?

Fill in each of the following blanks with the correct identification.

Early India

1. _____: Name used to refer to the entire subcontinent that encompasses modern-day Pakistan, India, Nepal, Bangladesh, and Sri Lanka.

2. _____: River valley in India where a civilization was established as early as 2500 B.C.E.

3. _____ and _____: Two urban centers of the first civilization in India.

4. _____: Sacred poetic writings that give a written record of early civilization (1500–500 B.C.E.) in India.

5. _____: Institution dividing Indian society into nobles, commoners, priests, workers, and untouchables.

6. _____: People who moved into the Indus River Valley area around 1900 B.C.E., as part of the great Indo-European migrations,

Early Society, Religion, and Culture

7. _____, _____, and _____: Three pillars of traditional Indian society.

8. _____: The Indo-European language introduced by the Aryans of the Indus Valley area.

9. _____: Cosmic Man of Vedic tradition, sacrificed to create the human world.

10. _____: Process by which the soul is reborn many times from one body to another.

11. _____: Those shunned by Indian society because they had defiling occupations.

12. _____: According to Vedic religion, the energy force that brought the world into being and kept the world going.

13. _____: One of the great Indian epics, it centers on the war between rivals for the throne of an Aryan state near modern Delhi.

14. _____: Epic that recounts the wanderings of Rama and Sita.

15. _____: Written during the Later Vedic Age, these speculations on the nature of reality formed the basis of Hindu religion and philosophy.

20

16. _____ : Legal texts in the Later Vedic Age, codified around 500 B.C.E., created to regulate Indian society.

Jainism, Buddhism, Hinduism

17. _____ : Concept that the most important duty a person has is to practice nonviolence and to cause no harm to any being.

18. _____ : Founder of Jainism.

19. _____ : The sense of right action, responsibility, or duty in Hinduism and Buddhism.

20. _____ : Buddhist approach to enlightenment between extreme asceticism and extreme self-indulgence.

21. _____ : "The Lord's Song," a philosophical dialogue stressing the performance of duty and overcoming passion and fear; it is still the most treasured piece in Hindu literature.

22. _____ : Persons who postpone their entry into final nirvana in order to be compassionate and loving guides to others still suffering in the world.

23. _____ : "Greater Vehicle" Buddhism that carried a message of hope and salvation for its followers.

Mauryan Empire, Other Kingdoms, and the Meeting of East and West

24. _____ : Founder of the Mauryan dynasty and India's first emperor.

25. _____ : Ardent Buddhist ruler who transformed Buddhism from a small Indian sect to an aggressive missionary faith.

26. _____ : Manual on government written for the Mauryan Empire.

27. _____ : City that produced Buddhist sculpture that was influenced by Greek art.

28. _____ : Descendants of the forces of Alexander the Great, these invaders established an independent kingdom in India about 245 B.C.E.

29. _____ : King of the Bactrian Greeks, he and his successors ruled an area that stretched from Bactria to the upper Ganges valley.

30. _____ : Nomads from central Asia who conquered the Punjab about 40 C.E. and whose rule gave India two centuries of peace and prosperity.

31. _____ : The large table plateau in south central India and home to the Dravidian peoples.

32. _____ : The term referring to the tradition of exquisite literature developed in the Tamil language in the south of India in the first few centuries of the Common Era.

33. _____ : Seasonal winds that blow off shore and on shore across India and determine much of its weather.

34. _____ and _____: Metals continually exported by the Romans to Asia to pay their adverse balance of trade.

35. _____: A statuette of this goddess, Vishnu's consort, was found in the ancient Roman city of Pompeii and stands as a symbol of the extensive contact between East and West in the first century C.E.

TRY THESE MULTIPLE-CHOICE QUESTIONS

1. _____ India's earliest civilization developed in the area of (1) the Deccan; (2) the Himalayas; (3) Hindustan; (4) the Malabar Coast; (5) Sri Lanka.

2. _____ Ancient civilizations of the Near East and India are similar in that all (1) were established by Indo-Europeans; (2) evolved with no contact from other cultures; (3) developed in great river valleys; (4) lasted over 2,000 years; (5) ended in sudden disaster.

3. _____ Which of the following occurred FIRST? (1) Aryan invasion of India; (2) birth of the Buddha; (3) building of Harappa; (4) beginning of the Early Vedic Age in India; (5) founding of the Mauryan Empire.

4. _____ Evidence of the Aryan invasion of India is shown by the (1) use of the stamp seal; (2) use of the potter's wheel; (3) introduction of metallurgy in Indian culture; (4) use of the stupa; (5) Sanskrit language.

5. _____ The Aryan migrations into India came (1) by sea; (2) across the Himalayas; (3) by caravan from Arabia; (4) from Southeast Asia; (5) through passes in the northwest mountains.

6. _____ Which of the following statements about the traditional Indian joint family is NOT true? (1) They were three generational households, a patriarchal system; (2) Group interests take precedence over individual needs; (3) Wives of the household's sons live in the household; (4) Males and females share equal inheritance rights; (5) They participated in leadership of the villages.

7. _____ The Mauryan Empire in India (1) set up elaborate administrative and court systems; (2) depended heavily on a professional army and secret police; (3) encouraged manufacturing, foreign trade, and agriculture; (4) made extensive use of diplomacy; (5) all of the above.

8. _____ Nirvana is (1) part of *samsura*; (2) the opposite of *moksha*; (3) results in *ahisma*; (4) another way to say brahman; (5) none of the above.

9. _____ Buddhism rejected all of the following EXCEPT (1) a pantheon of gods; (2) the Brahmin priestly elite; (3) the caste system; (4) reincarnation; (5) nonviolence.

10. _____ The ancient Indus Valley civilization included all of the following EXCEPT (1) the cultivation of cereals; (2) an alphabetic written language; (3) domesticated animals; (4) urban living and intercity trade; (5) large population centers.

11. _____ The Dravidians were (1) Hindu priests; (2) an Indian ethnic group displaced by the Aryans; (3) a Hindu warrior caste; (4) elite Mauryan warriors; (5) none of the above.

12. _____ Members of the highest Hindu caste were the (1) priests; (2) warriors; (3) farmers; (4) merchants; (5) tanners.

22

13. _____ Aryan religious practice involved all of the following EXCEPT (1) sacrifices; (2) priestly ritual; (3) worship of one god; (4) belief that gods controlled the laws of nature; (5) recitation of hymns.

14. _____ The priestly class of the Aryans is called (1) Vedas; (2) Brahmanas; (3) *Upanishads*; (4) Brahmans; (5) Rajas.

15. _____ The *Upanishads* introduced all of the following ideas EXCEPT (1) the concept of *jiva*; (2) you are continually reborn; (3) you are marked by your deeds in the next life; (4) *moksha* is the only escape from rebirth; (5) *Brahman* is the only permanent reality.

16. _____ Jains and Buddhists share belief in (1) a single god; (2) nonviolence; (3) Vedic scripture; (4) spreading a religious message internationally; (5) a heaven and a hell.

17. _____ Jains evolved into scholars and merchants because (1) by 300 B.C.E. trade was growing in India; (2) women were allowed to pursue *moksha*; (3) all beings feel pain; (4) farming was forbidden to them; (5) they had become a majority.

18. _____ Buddhism (1) renounces extreme asceticism; (2) had a single founder; (3) offers therapy for individual unhappiness; (4) is open to everyone; (5) all of the above.

19. _____ The root cause of human unhappiness in Buddhism is (1) sin; (2) craving; (3) poverty; (4) sexual deprivation; (5) lack of pride.

20. _____ The four Aryan castes defined in the Vedas were called (1) karma; (2) samsara; (3) varna; (4) dharma; (5) jina.

MAKING CONNECTIONS

*This exercise compares the three ancient religions of India: Hinduism, Jainism, and Buddhism. Beside each item, place an **H** for Hinduism, **J** for Jainism, or **B** for Buddhism, depending on which is appropriate.*

1. _____ Believed everything is one in *Brahman*.

2. _____ Suggested that nirvana came through strict discipline of mind and body.

3. _____ Worshipped many gods.

4. _____ Sought to avoid causing harm or pain to any creature.

5. _____ Its founder was enlightened under a tree.

6. _____ Originated the practice of yoga.

7. _____ Maintains permanent occupational classifications.

8. _____ Invokes the gods through ritual and sacrifice.

9. _____ Monks wear yellow robes and carry begging bowls.

10. _____ Holds that all beings have souls.

11. _____ The only religion to spread beyond India.

12. _____ Taught the Four Noble Truths.

13. _____ *Mantras* from the scriptures will cure diseases.

14. _____ Ashoka's favored religion.

15. _____ Its religious values are emphasized in long epic poems.

DO YOU KNOW THE SIGNIFICANCE OF THESE TERMS?

This chapter contains some terms that may be unfamiliar, but they represent important events and tendencies in world history. In the space provided, identify each of the following and evaluate its historical significance.

sindhu

Mohenjo-Daro

castes

Aryans

Dravidians

Dharma

Sangha

Rig-Veda

Jainism

Hindu Synthesis

Noble Eightfold Path

Arthasastra

Ashoka

Mahabharata

Kushanas

THE PLACE

On the map below, locate and label these places, using the maps in the text chapter.

India	Bactria	Indus River	Red Sea
Bay of Bengal	Aden	Arabia	Parthia
Arabian Sea	Africa	Tamil Land	Petra
Persian Gulf	Pacific Ocean	Tibet	Taxila
Himalaya Mts.	Vindhya Mts.	Khyber Pass	Ceylon (Sri Lanka)

A. *Use a solid line to trace a feasible land route from Taxila in India to the eastern Mediterranean and Rome.*

B. *Use dashed lines to trace the water routes by which Buddhism spread to Southeast Asia and by which Buddhism spread to China.*

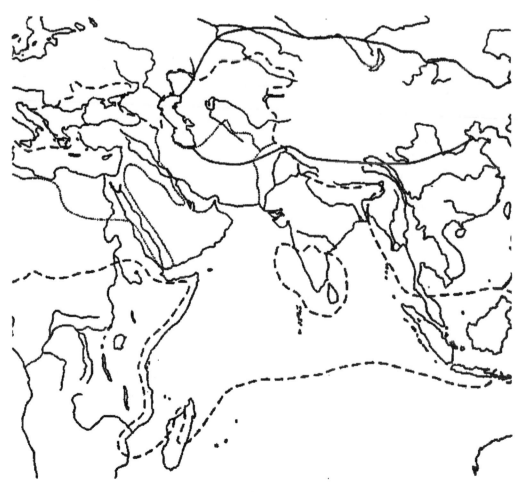

RELATIONSHIPS IN TIME

Events in the earliest river civilizations and in the ancient history of the Near East, China, and India often ran parallel. Using what you have learned in the preceding chapters, place the items below in the appropriate column and chronological position on the time line below. Alongside the lines, bracket and label the indicated time periods. (Some of the items will overlap with others, since one of the objectives of time lines is to point out what was going on in various parts of the world in a particular era.)

Indus Valley civilization

Aryan invasion

Later Vedic Age

Mauryan dynasty

Siddhartha Gautama

King David

First Emperor

Warring States

Zoroastrianism

Phoenicians

Kushana Empire

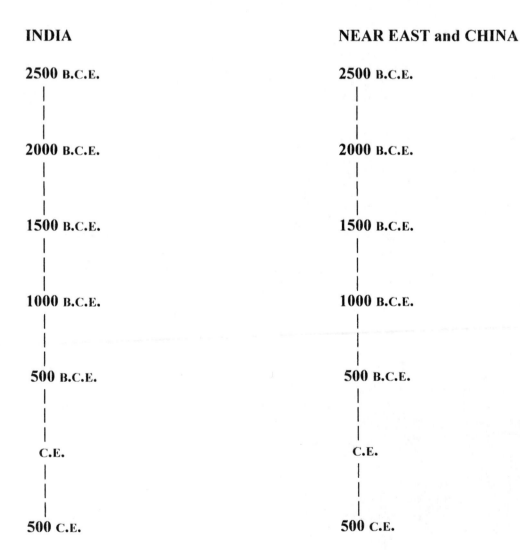

INDIA

2500 B.C.E.

2000 B.C.E.

1500 B.C.E.

1000 B.C.E.

500 B.C.E.

C.E.

500 C.E.

NEAR EAST and CHINA

2500 B.C.E.

2000 B.C.E.

1500 B.C.E.

1000 B.C.E.

500 B.C.E.

C.E.

500 C.E.

ARRIVING AT CONCLUSIONS

Here are some quotations from eminent historians dealing with the significance of this period of history. Answer the accompanying questions briefly and be prepared to defend your position.

1. "Caste moderates personal ambitions and checks the bitterness of competition. It gives a man, whatever his station in life, a society in which he can be at home even when he is among strangers. For the poor man, it serves as a club, a trade union and a mutual benevolent society, all rolled into one. It ensures continuity and a certain inherited skill in the arts and crafts. And in the moral sphere it means that every man lives content with that place which Destiny has allotted to him, and uncomplainingly does his best." (Lord Meston, *Nationhood for India* [New Haven: Yale University Press, 1931], p. 50.)

Do the advantages of caste cited above outweigh the disadvantages of a stratified society? Why will modern industrialization make it difficult for caste to persist in the long run? In the short run, how does caste make modernization more difficult for India?

2. "Ashoka was hailed as the first true . . . universal emperor of India. He addressed all Indians as 'my children' and carved in stone his paternalistic administration's express desire 'that they may obtain every kind of welfare and happiness both in this world and the next.' Ashoka was said to have informed his subordinates . . . that no matter where he was . . . he was always 'on duty' to carry out the 'business' of state. . . . In his twenty-sixth year, the emperor inscribed the following message: 'Both this world and the other are hard to reach, except by great love of the law, great self-examination, great obedience, great respect, great energy. . . . This is my rule: government by the law, administration according to the law, gratification of my subjects under the law, and protection through the law.' Ashoka abandoned the traditional annual royal hunt in favor of a 'pilgrimage of religious law' which allowed him to visit distant corners of his empire personally, the living symbol of imperial unity to his people." (Stanley Wolpert, *A New History of India* [New York: Oxford University Press, 1977], pp. 63, 66–67.)

What are the various qualities that this ideal ruler exhibited? Would such qualities have validity in a political leader today? Would there be room for the growth of a spirit of democratic self-sufficiency in such a political environment? How would Lord Shang compare (see Chapter 2)?

QUESTIONS TO THINK ABOUT

1. From what you have seen in civilizations in the Fertile Crescent and China, what characteristics are similar to those of the Indus River Valley civilization? What characteristics are different?

2. How did the trade connections between India, the Middle East, and China have a significant impact on these civilizations?

3. What is it about rivers that encourages the rise of civilizations, as in the Indus River Valley, Yellow River Valley, Mesopotamia, and Egypt?

4. When the Mauryan Empire united most of India under one government, how did it benefit the people? Does an empire benefit everyone or only those at the top?

27

CHAPTER 4

Greece: Minoan, Mycenaean, Hellenic, and Hellenistic Civilizations, 2000–30 B.C.E.

The Hellenic peoples, better known to us today as the Greeks, by the late fourth century B.C.E. changed the world forever, particularly the West. Their inquisitiveness, experimentation, dedication to harmony, balance and moderation, and quest for excellence left an enduring legacy. The Greek search to answer some of the most profound questions of the human experience and their heroic striving for perfection in the face of obvious limitations would echo across the ages. In philosophy, science, politics, literature, and art and architecture, in spite of their shortcomings, the Greeks did much to define the set of values we have come to know as "classical."

Hellenistic, or "Greek-like" Macedonians, led by the conquering kings Philip II and Alexander the Great and his successors, swept across the map, through the Greek isles and east to the Indus River, spreading Greek values and practices. This diffusion of Greek influence, "Hellenism," in economics and scientific and intellectual achievement was characterized by a new cosmopolitanism, which guaranteed that the complex of Greek values, good and bad, would provide the bedrock for civilization in the West and would have an important impact eastward to India.

YOU SHOULD HAVE A BASIC UNDERSTANDING OF:

Minoan and Mycenaean cultures and their influence on classical Greece.

Hellenic Greece—its political history and its astonishing cultural achievements, culminating in the classical age.

How Greek culture was diffused and its life extended during the Hellenistic era.

HAVE YOU MASTERED THE BASIC FACTS?

Fill in each of the following blanks with the correct identification.

Minoan and Mycenaean Civilizations

1. _____: Island people whose civilization influenced the cultural development of the early Mycenaean Greeks.

2. _____: First Indo-European tribes to migrate into Greece.

3. _____: Dominant city of the Minoan civilization in the middle of the second millennium.

4. _____: Palace built of brick and limestone, with running water, sanitation system, and elaborate frescoes, it provides helpful insights into Minoan society and culture.

5. _____: Excavated by Schliemann in 1876, this city on the mainland of Greece gave its name to an early Greek civilization.

6. _____: English archaeologist who excavated the remains of the great civilization on the island of Crete.

7. _____: According to scholars, the fabled city of Troy has been unearthed at this archaeological site.

8. _____: Intriguing Minoan script that has 87 signs representing symbols but has not been deciphered.

9. _____: Modern-day location of the spectacular eruption in 1628 B.C.E. of the volcanic island Thera, which led to the downfall of the Minoans.

The Hellenic Age

10. _____: Greek hero, credited with bringing the first humans to inhabit Greece, whose name provides the origin for the term "Hellenic."

11. _____: Foreign power that sent a military expedition against Greece in 490 B.C.E. and made a second attempt to conquer Greece about a decade later.

12. _____: Age from about 1150 to 750 B.C.E., named for a great epic poet or poets whose works portray the life of the period.

13. _____: Greek name for a city-state, the basic political unit of the Greeks.

14. _____: "Government by the few."

15. _____: Greek term for "excellence" or "virtue."

16. _____: Battle for a narrow pass in Greece where a small band of Spartans and a few thousand Greek allies held up the vast Persian army in a delaying action.

17. _____: Greek city of totalitarian ideals, ruled rigidly by a military faction whose every word was law.

18. _____: Term for the Spartan saying, "Come back *with* your shield or *on* it."

19. _____: Leader whose idealism has been cited as being mainly responsible for establishing democracy.

20. _____: Athenian politician in the sixth century B.C.E. whose reforms have made his name synonymous with wise statecraft.

21. _____: What fate follows the sin of hubris.

22. _____: Athenian statesman who instituted democratic ideals and dominated Greek politics during the Golden Age."

23. _____: Greek civil war that destroyed the military power of Athens.

Greek Genius

24. _____: Important Greek historian who described the clash of the Hellenic and Near Eastern cultures.

25. _____: Often called the "father of philosophy," whose speculations led him to conclude that the basic substance of the universe was water.

26. _____: First "scientific historian" and the author of an objective history of the Peloponnesian War.

27. _____: Early mathematician-philosopher who held that the universe was founded on mathematical principles.

28. _____: Thinker who first advanced an atomic theory to explain the composition of the universe.

29. _____: Athenian-born philosopher who sought the truth by asking questions and then subjecting the answers to rigorous logical analysis.

30. _____: Founder of the Athenian Academy, famous for his emphasis on the Ideal and for writing the *Republic*.

31. _____: The philosopher-tutor of Alexander the Great; authoritative writer on a host of subjects, whose works were standard in the Middle Ages.

32. _____: Greek physician, famous for his use of observation in medicine and for his code of medical ethics.

33. _____: Playwright in Greek legend who added a character to Greek dramas called "the answerer" ("hypocrites") to converse with the chorus and its leader.

34. _____: Greece's greatest comic dramatist of Athenian folkways.

35. _____: According to Aristotle, the kind of virtue that is most important for society.

36. _____: The most famous fifth-century B.C.E. Greek sculptor whose work is characterized by charm, grace, and individuality.

The Hellenistic Age

37. _____: "Greek-like."

38. _____: Fourth-century Macedonian king whose military conquests brought unity to Greece on the eve of his own assassination.

39. _____: His father was an accomplished warrior, his mother was a princess who told him his real father was Zeus, and he carried his copy of the *Iliad* wherever he traveled; he became a "warrior philosopher."

40. _____: Ruler of Egypt after the death of Alexander the Great.

41. _____: Hellenistic philosophy that sought tranquility of soul through indifference to pain, pleasure, and all human emotions; advocated withdrawal from society.

42. _____: School of philosophy founded by Zeno of Cyprus, which held that the wise person would accept without complaint whatever fate allotted; advocated participation in society.

43. _____: Hellenistic astronomer who suggested a heliocentric theory of the solar system.

44. _____: Cynic philosopher who wandered unattached from city to city.

45. _____: He calculated the circumference of the globe within one percent by measuring the difference in angles of the noonday sun's shadows at Aswan and Alexandria.

46. _____: Hellenistic city that was a major commercial center and was home to some of the ancient world's most precious treasures, including an imposing lighthouse and a magnificent library.

47. _____: Highly decorative form of capital, or crown, of Greek columns, with carved leaves and scrolls characteristic of the period.

TRY THESE MULTIPLE-CHOICE QUESTIONS

1. _____ A legendary ruler of Crete during the early development of Greek civilization was (1) Plutarch; (2) Antigonid; (3) Minos; (4) Pylos; (5) Menes.

2. _____ One obstacle to increasing our knowledge of the civilization of ancient Crete has been (1) the reluctance of modern Cretans to discuss their ancestors; (2) the failure of the Cretans to develop a written language; (3) a lack of interest in the subject by modern scholars; (4) our inability to decipher all types of Cretan written language; (5) none of the above.

3. _____ An *acropolis* was originally (1) a fortified center of a Greek city; (2) a member of a priesthood; (3) a shrine to Zeus on Mount Olympus; (4) a commercial center; (5) none of the above.

4. _____ *Magna Graecia* is the name applied to (1) any Greek city-state tyrant; (2) Greek colonies in Sicily and southern Italy; (3) the cultural achievements of the Hellenic Age; (4) black and red Greek pottery; (5) distinctive columns at the Parthenon.

5. _____ The Persian ruler defeated by Alexander the Great was (1) Xerxes; (2) Ptolemy; (3) Hermes; (4) Darius III; (5) Cyrus IV.

6. _____ Which of the following did NOT become a part of Alexander's empire? (1) Parthia; (2) Media; (3) Arabia; (4) Egypt; (5) Greece.

7. _____ Greek sculpture in the archaic period shows a strong influence of the style of (1) China; (2) Egypt; (3) India; (4) Sumeria; (5) Persia.

8. _____ A Greek dramatist whose plays stressed themes of divine justice, morality, and ethics was (1) Hermes; (2) Zeus; (3) Thales of Miletus; (4) Sophocles; (5) Aristophanes.

9. _____ The Greek writer whose *Oresteia* explored the disastrous effects of hubris and the destructive results of the blood feud was (1) Aeschylus; (2) Hesiod; (3) Euripedes; (4) Sophocles; (5) Homer.

10. _____ In contrast to other ancient civilizations, that of the Minoans (1) was less concerned with economic activity; (2) was more isolationist and less interested in contacts with other peoples; (3) allowed women much greater freedom and dignity; (4) none of the above; (5) all of the above.

11. _____ Government during the Homeric Age can best be described as (1) aristocratic; (2) democratic; (3) tyrannical; (4) anarchical; (5) oligarchical.

12. _____ The story of the *Iliad* centers on a conflict between (1) Achaeans and Minoans; (2) Sparta and Athens; (3) Achaeans and Trojans; (4) Achaeans and Persians; (5) Athenians and Macedonians.

13. _____ An Athenian building, built to house a statue of Athena and regarded as a classic example of visually perfect architecture, is the (1) Erechtheum; (2) Parthenon; (3) Acropolis; (4) Propylaea; (5) Agora.

14. _____ The legendary lawgiver of Sparta was (1) Euripedes; (2) Lycurgus; (3) Diogenes; (4) Solon; (5) Cleisthenes.

15. _____ The supposed home of Zeus, the king of the gods, was (1) Melos; (2) Delos; (3) Athens; (4) Olympus; (5) none of the above.

16. _____ Spartan society was noted for (1) its emphasis on democracy; (2) promotion of travel to other lands; (3) its military character; (4) dedication to religious beliefs; (5) none of the above.

17. _____ The Delian League was (1) originally a defensive alliance formed by Athens; (2) a military alliance headed by Sparta; (3) the political organ of the Olympic games; (4) an anti-Trojan alliance formed by the Mycenaeans; (5) a free trade union of all Greek city-states.

18. _____ The Athenian tyrant who promoted cultural and economic progress during his reign was (1) Aristophanes; (2) Isocrates; (3) Dionysus; (4) Pericles; (5) none of the above.

19. _____ The institution of *ostracism* was the practice of (1) benevolent despotism; (2) sending citizens into exile by popular vote; (3) promoting civic pride through military aggression; (4) philosophical moderation; (5) censorship of social critics.

20. _____ Tombs built in a beehive-like shape were a feature of the culture of the (1) Trojans; (2) Minoans; (3) Mycenaeans; (4) Spartans; (5) Ionians.

21. _____ Choose by number the correct generalizations regarding contrasts between Sparta and Athens: (a) Unlike Athens, Sparta devoted little attention to foreign trade and cultural contacts; (b) Sparta expanded by conquering adjacent areas instead of following the Athenian practice of colonization; (c) Unlike Athens, Sparta placed security, political conservatism, and military strength above cultural creativity and social progress; (d) Sparta encouraged its citizens to travel abroad and bring back new ideas, instead of following the Athenian model of restricting contacts with other peoples. (1) a and d; (2) a, b, and c; (3) only d; (4) b and c; (5) none of the above.

22. _____ Which of the following occurred FIRST? (1) Persian Wars; (2) Peloponnesian War; (3) Trojan War; (4) Alexander's conquest of Persia; (5) Mycenaen conquest of Crete.

23. _____ Which of the following occurred FIRST? (1) formation of the Delian League; (2) Homer's *Odyssey* put into written form; (3) Age of Oligarchy; (4) reforms of Solon; (5) rule of Pericles.

24. _____ Characteristics of Hellenistic culture included (1) increased realism and emotional content of sculpture; (2) significant advances in geography and mathematics; (3) cosmopolitanism; (4) spread of trade connecting East and West; (5) all of the above.

25. _____ During the seventh century B.C.E., Athenian nobles erected a governing system in which the king's authority was exercised by magistrates called (1) tyrants; (2) Sophists; (3) archons; (4) Eleusinians; (5) elders.

MAKING CONNECTIONS: ATHENS vs. SPARTA

Although they were both Greek city-states, Athens and Sparta were very different in many ways. In each blank, put either an A to indicate a characteristic of Athens or an S to indicate Sparta.

1. _____ Economy based on trade and colonization.

2. _____ Solon's ideals of moderation and justice.

3. _____ Militaristic totalitarian state.

4. _____ Individuals had to subordinate themselves to the state.

5. _____ Golden Age under Pericles.

6. _____ Residents of Messenia who were forced by the Spartans to become state slaves.

7. _____ Voting privileges extended to all adult male citizens.

8. _____ Culturally and economically isolated.

9. _____ Unparalleled flowering in the arts and philosophy.

10. _____ Allied with other oligarchic city-states.

11. _____ Allied with other democratic city-states.

12. _____ Ban on trade and travel led to isolation and intellectual stagnation.

13. _____ Boys lived under rigorous military discipline from the age of seven.

14. _____ Girls participated in athletic events.

RELATIONSHIPS IN TIME

Write in the dates for each of the periods on the chart below. Under these headings, place the items that belong there chronologically.

Persian Wars
Linear B script
Stoicism
Parthenon
Delian League
Ptolemaic rulers in Egypt
Aeschylus
Aristarchus
Iliad and *Odyssey*
Trojan War
Seleucid rulers in the Persian Empire
Sophocles
Socrates
Alexander the Great
Battle of Marathon
Palace of Knossos

Sappho of Lesbos
Cretan Mother Goddess
Solon
Euripides
Skeptics and Cynics
Philip II conquered the Greek city-states
Antigonus the One-Eyed
Thales of Miletus
Pericles
Peloponnesian War
Hesiod's *Works and Days*
Praxiteles
Pisistratus
Cleisthenes
Greek culture diffused throughout the ancient
        East and the Roman West

Minoan Period   _____

Mycenaean Period   _____

Homeric Age
(Greek Dark Ages)   _____

Age of Oligarchy   _____

Classical Period   _____

Hellenistic Age   _____

DO YOU KNOW THE SIGNIFICANCE OF THESE TERMS?

In Chapter 4, these terms represent important aspects of world history. In the space provided, identify each of the following and evaluate its historical significance.

Linear B

Homer

hubris

polis

Solon

laconic farewell

Aspasia

Peloponnesian War

Greek miracle

Plato

Pericles

Parthenon

Library of Alexandria

Archimedes

Stoics

THE PLACE

On the following outline map, write in the name of each of the following items in the correct location.

Sea of Marmara
Black Sea
Hellespont
Aegean Sea
Ionia

Ionian Sea
Peloponnesus
Macedonia
Adriatic Sea
Persian Empire

For each item, write the place name that fits the definition both in the blank and on the map.

1. _____: Center of an early Indo-European culture on the Greek mainland.

2. _____: City besieged by Greeks as described in the *Iliad*.

3. _____: Part of Magna Graecia and Sicily.

4. _____: Greek city-state Solon and Pisistratus helped reform.

5. _____: Militaristic city-state where a totalitarian society ruled over a subject population of helots.

6. _____: Site of battle in 338 B.C.E. where the Macedonians under Philip II forced their hegemony on the Greek city-states.

7. _____: Athens won this decisive battle with the powerful Persians in 490 B.C.E.

ARRIVING AT CONCLUSIONS

Here are some quotations from eminent historians dealing with aspects of Greek history. Answer the accompanying questions briefly and be prepared to defend your position.

1. "It is sometimes asserted that this system of independent poleis was imposed on Greece by the physical character of the country. The theory is attractive, especially to those who like to have one majestic explanation of any phenomenon, but it does not seem to be true. It is of course obvious that the physical subdivision of the country helped; the system could not have existed, for example, in Egypt, a country which depends entirely on the proper management of the Nile flood, and therefore must have a central government. But there are countries cut up quite as much as Greece—Scotland, for instance—which have never developed the polis system; and conversely there were in Greece many neighboring poleis, such as Corinth and Sicyon, which remained independent of each other although between them there was no physical barrier that would seriously incommode a modern cyclist. Moreover, it was precisely the most mountainous parts of Greece that never developed poleis, or not until later days—Arcadia and Aetolia, for example, which had something like a canton system. The polis flourished in those parts where communications were relatively easy." (H. D. F. Kitto, *The Greeks* [Baltimore: Penguin Books, 1959], p. 69.)

What different kinds of evidence does Kitto offer to support his contention that geography does not give an adequate explanation for the evolution of the Greek polis as the basic political unit? Does he deny that geography had any influence in this process? Kitto argues that the real explanation for the development and survival of the polis can be found in the character of the Greeks. What aspects of Greek character do you think might help explain the polis? Do you think the authors of *Civilization Past & Present* would agree with this quotation? Why or why not?

2. "The Greeks gave to the world their purity and grace, their ease and joy of life, their physical beauty, their intellectual fire, and their sense of the dignity of man under the heavens, but they gave far more. They gave us a way of life which we have largely followed, often without realizing that we are treading in their footsteps. They were the superb artificers of a civilization which has endured for so long that we are in danger of forgetting that they are our parents. They thought the thoughts we are still thinking, and dreamed the dreams we are still dreaming. They throw their long shadows over us, and to our surprise we discover that these shadows are made of beams of intense light; for they came at the dawn, and we are still far from high noon." (Robert Payne, *Ancient Greece, the Triumph of a Culture* [New York: Norton, 1964], p. 434.)

What thoughts are we still thinking that the ancient Greeks thought? What aspects of the Greek way of life can you identify in your society today? Do you agree with Payne's conclusion that civilization today is still "far from high noon"? Why or why not?

3. In a famous funeral oration early in the Peloponnesian War, Pericles describes how the Athenians acquired a great empire: "The administration [of the city] is in the hands of the many and not of the few. . . . There is no exclusiveness in our public life and in our private intercourse we are not suspicious of one another, nor angry with our neighbor if he does what he likes. . . . A spirit of reverence pervades our public acts; we are prevented from doing wrong by respect for authority and for the laws, having especial regard for those which are for the protection of the injured as well as to those unwritten laws [upheld by] the general sentiment." (Thucydides, *History of the Peloponnesian War* [trans. Benjamin Jowett], 2nd rev. ed. [Oxford: Clarendon Press], vol. 1, pp. 127–128.)

What does Pericles mean by "those unwritten laws"? Are they valid today? In what measure is Pericles portraying the reality of Athenian democracy?

QUESTIONS TO THINK ABOUT

1. How is the importance of geography reflected in the political development of Greece?

2. From the fourth to the second centuries B.C.E., how did Greek culture come to be widely spread? What was the significance of this diffusion?

3. What part did the Minoan and Mycenaean cultures play in linking Greek civilization with that of the Near East?

4. One often hears of the American way of life. Sum up that of the Greeks (as reflected by Athens) by listing six or more of its basic characteristics, explaining and evaluating each.

5. The Greeks championed nonconformity and freedom of thought. Do you think this legacy is in danger today? Where and why? Are there limits to an individual's nonconformity and freedom of expression? Where would you draw the line?

6. What might be the lesson of Greek political individualism to the nations of western Europe today?

7. What were the greatest contributions of the Greeks in art, architecture, literature, and philosophy? Explain your answer.

8. Although the Hellenistic period was relatively short, it had an important impact on world history. Do you agree or disagree? Please explain your response.

CHAPTER 5

Roman Civilization: The Roman World, c. 900 B.C.E. to 476 C.E.

Emerging out of the Etruscan experience, the inhabitants of Rome developed a republic by the late sixth century B.C.E. Over the next one thousand years, the civilization there developed into an empire the likes of which the world has not seen since. It was an unplanned empire shaped by circumstance and by practical, pragmatic administrators, military leaders, and politicians who were great admirers of classical values of the Hellenized world. In the process of moving from republic to empire, the Romans changed their society and culture, assimilating and diffusing as they conquered civilizations from Britain to Bethlehem.

The Romans had great writers, poets, historians, and scientists. But their real genius lay in law, administration, engineering, and military prowess. Their empire provided the incubator for the growth of a new religion, Christianity, which would survive even the Romans. In the end, the world's most famous empire, which represented a high point in human political achievement, would collapse and wither unceremoniously away, leaving us to ponder the reasons why and to reflect on Roman contributions to future generations.

YOU SHOULD HAVE A BASIC UNDERSTANDING OF:

The different peoples that came into the Italian peninsula and their influence on Rome.

The steps by which the ordinary people gained political rights and power.

Specifically how and when Rome built its empire.

The civil wars of the late empire.

The benefits of the Roman peace, the *Pax Romana*.

The political and religious circumstances into which Jesus was born, the efforts and persecution of his early converts, and their eventual success in shaping the early church.

The role of Christian monasteries and missionaries in preserving and extending Greco-Roman civilization.

Germanic tribes and Germanic invasions.

The economic, social, cultural, political, and military factors that contributed to the decline and collapse of Roman power.

The legacy of Rome in terms of law, politics, engineering, architecture, and the writing of history.

HAVE YOU MASTERED THE BASIC FACTS?

Fill in each of the following blanks with the correct identification.

Italy and Rome to 509 B.C.E.

1. _____: Mountain chain that runs most of the length of the Italian peninsula.

2. _____ and _____: Legendary twin brothers who, tradition says, were the founders of Rome.

3. _____: Early, highly advanced people who settled north of Rome and ruled the Romans for almost a century.

4. _____: A group of Indo-Europeans who settled in the lower valley of the Tiber River.

5. _____: According to legend, Rome was linked to Greece through this Trojan hero who, after the fall of Troy, founded a settlement in Latium.

6. _____: Name given to the symbol of executive power (*imperium*) of Rome's king, represented by an ax bound in a bundle of birch rods.

7. _____: The council of nobles who advised the king and whose members belonged to the patrician class.

The Early Republic: 509–133 B.C.E.

8. _____: Greek king who defeated Rome in a battle that fatally weakened his forces, an event that gave rise to the use of his name to describe any over-costly victory.

9. _____: "Gathering of the plebians," it was an assembly presided over by tribunes, which became known as the Tribal Assembly and in 287 B.C.E. was authorized to pass laws binding on all citizens.

10. _____: Three wars between Carthage and Rome, in which Carthage was utterly destroyed.

11. _____: Carthaginian military genius and inspiring leader who tried vainly to defeat Rome.

12. _____: Roman general who finally matched the skill of the Carthaginian military genius described above and defeated the forces of Carthage at Zama in Africa.

13. _____: Title given to the father of the family, whose power was absolute and was used to promote self-control, loyalty, courage, respect for laws, and ancestral customs.

The Late Republic: 133–30 B.C.E.

14. _____: Two brothers who, as tribunes, tried hard to solve Rome's social and economic problems in the second century B.C.E. but were thwarted by an unyielding Senate.

15. _____: Brilliant general and statesman who realized opportunities to advance himself politically during the late republic, seized power (49 B.C.E.) and was later assassinated.

16. _____ : General who emerged victorious in the first civil war and who was appointed dictator by the Senate in 82 B.C.E. for an unlimited term.

17. _____ : Large slave plantations that replaced most small farms by the first century B.C.E.

The Early Empire: 30 B.C.E.–180 C.E.

18. _____ : Grandnephew of Julius Caesar, creator of the Roman Empire, and brilliant ruler; better known as Augustus.

19. _____ : Infamous emperor of the first century C.E., who began persecution of Christians in Rome.

20. _____ : Nephew and successor to Tiberius, he was a megalomaniac who considered having his favorite horse elected to high office in Rome.

21. _____ : Period of approximately 200 years during which the Romans controlled and maintained peace within their empire.

22. _____ : Last and perhaps best-known of the "five good emperors," famous for his advocacy of Stoic philosophy.

23. _____ : Huge Roman arena for gladiatorial combats that opened in 80 C.E.

24. _____ : City buried by an eruption of Vesuvius, whose remains have given us a picture of Roman home and urban life.

The Rise and Triumph of Christianity

25. _____ : Militant Jewish communal group that practiced the monastic way of life before Christianity.

26. _____ : Founder of Jewish sect based on belief in the Messiah; reports of his teachings and miracles spread quickly among the Jews as he and his 12 disciples traveled from village to village.

27. _____ : Greatest missionary of early Christianity, active about 35 to 65 C.E.

28. _____ : Persons who voluntarily suffer death rather than deny their religious convictions as did many Christians during days of persecution by Roman authorities.

29. _____ : Emperor who issued a decree granting toleration to Christians and who moved the capitol of the Roman Empire to the old Greek colony of Byzantium.

30. _____ : Emperor who made Christianity the official religion of the Roman Empire.

31. _____ : Title for the religious leader of a diocese.

32. _____ : Founder of Western monasticism and author of famous monastic rules.

33. _____ : Author of *Confessions*, fifth-century bishop of Hippo in North Africa, and the author of numerous religious works that became the foundation of much of the theology of Western Christianity.

43

34. _____ : Meeting of church leaders in 325, which concluded that Arianism was a heresy and endorsed the concept of the Trinity.

35. _____ : Fifth-century pope during whose pontificate Rome achieved its position of primacy in the Western church.

Rome in Crisis, Germanic Invasions

36. _____ : Site of the decisive battle in which a Roman army was defeated by the Visigoths in 376 B.C.E.

37. _____ : Called the "scourge of God," this warlord of the Huns mounted a threat to Rome in 451 C.E. but was defeated at Troyes by a combined force of Romans and Visigoths.

38. _____ : Term denoting absolute rule of Roman emperor.

39. _____ : In 476, he was deposed, becoming the last Roman emperor in the West.

40. _____ : The German leader who set up a vast Ostrogothic kingdom in Italy, with his capital at Ravenna.

The Roman Legacy

41. _____ : Inscribed on a dozen bronze tablets and set up publicly in the Forum, it was the first landmark development in the long history of Roman law.

42. _____ : Probably the best-known Roman poet; author of the *Aeneid*.

43. _____ : Historian of the first and second centuries C.E., whose works glorified the simple virtues of the German tribes in contrast to the pervasive corruption and decadence of Roman society.

44. _____ : Stone structure consisting of a connected series of tiers of arches topped by a water channel.

45. _____ : Greatest orator and most polished Latin stylist of Caesar's day.

46. _____ and _____ : Two systems of Greek philosophy especially popular in Rome.

47. _____ : Prominent geographer and astronomer of Alexandria whose views, right and wrong, dominated medieval European thought.

48. _____ : Most famous Greek author in the Roman Empire; his best-known work is *Parallel Lives*.

49. _____ : Roman building that remains today the most impressive example of the use of the dome by Roman architects.

50. _____ : Physician who first explained the biological mechanism of respiration and who compiled an encyclopedia that summarized ancient medical knowledge.

TRY THESE MULTIPLE-CHOICE QUESTIONS

1. _____ The first wave of Indo-European invaders of Italy settled in the valley of the (1) Po; (2) Tiber; (3) Arno; (4) Rubicon; (5) Rhone.

2. _____ A comparison of the Roman Forum with the Greek Acropolis suggests that the Romans (1) gave higher priority to governmental and other secular affairs than did the Greeks; (2) borrowed heavily from Greek architectural styles; (3) made extensive use of the arch, vaults and domes; (4) readily borrowed ideas from other people; (5) all of the above.

3. _____ From the Etruscans, the Romans borrowed all of the following EXCEPT (1) the arch; (2) the alphabet; (3) the Etruscan language; (4) religious beliefs; (5) treatment of women.

4. _____ The Greek scientist famous for his compilation of medical knowledge and for his emphasis on experimentation was (1) Galen; (2) Cicero; (3) Ptolemy; (4) Strabo; (5) Horace.

5. _____ The Roman poet whose collections of myths preserved classical mythology for the modern world through his *Metamorphoses* was (1) Virgil; (2) Ovid; (3) Juvenal; (4) Homer; (5) Juvenal.

6. _____ Which of the following was NEVER a part of the Roman Empire? (1) Macedonia; (2) Spain; (3) Poland; (4) Tunisia; (5) Gaul.

7. _____ Which of the following was NOT the name of a leading Roman literary figure? (1) Horace; (2) Plautus; (3) Catullus; (4) Scipio; (5) Pliny.

8. _____ Roman sculpture was characterized by (1) idealized portrayals of general types; (2) crudity and an unwillingness to learn from Greek masters; (3) realistic portraiture; (4) extensive use of bronze; (5) none of the above.

9. _____ The largest Roman domed structure and the oldest massive roofed building in the world that is still intact is: (1) the Colosseum; (2) the Parthenon; (3) the Pantheon; (4) the Hippodrome; (5) none of the above.

10. _____ Which of the following occurred FIRST? (1) Roman conquest of Sicily; (2) formation of the Latin League; (3) Roman conquest of Greece; (4) First Punic War; (5) the Samnite Wars.

11. _____ Compared with the Greeks, the Romans (1) were more concerned with engineering and practical applications of architecure; (2) were less practical and more inclined to other worldly pursuits; (3) were more frivolous and inclined to anarchy; (4) did not like to borrow ideas from others; (5) all of the above.

12. _____ Choose the number at the end of this question that correctly identifies the characteristics of Roman government and political philosophy during the reign of the Antonine emperors: (a) weak and corrupt emperors; (b) represented the height of imperial power and prosperity; (c) emperors sharing authority with the Senate; (d) paramount importance of the rule of law. (1) b, c, and d; (2) only c; (3) a and b; (4) only d; (5) a, b, c, and d.

13. _____ The Appian Way (1) connected Rome and the Po River; (2) connected Rome and the Bay of Naples; (3) ended at the English Channel; (4) ran from Rome to the provinces in Spain; (5) linked the Po and Tiber Rivers.

14. _____ A Roman emperor noted for his adherence to Stoicism and who preferred the study of philosophy to the glory of the battlefield was (1) Julius Caesar; (2) Pliny the Elder; (3) Marcus Aurelius; (4) Seneca; (5) Titus.

15. _____ Which of the following did Octavian defeat in battle, thus winning uncontested control of Rome's empire? (1) Antony; (2) Pompey; (3) Cicero; (4) Marius and Sulla; (5) Crassus.

16. _____ The attempted reforms of the Gracchi aimed at (1) rebuilding the Roman army and navy; (2) protecting the rights of businesses in foreign countries; (3) restoring independence and prosperity to the small farmer; (4) restoring the power of the Senate; (5) all of the above.

17. _____ Which of the following was NOT a noteworthy historian during the Republic or Empire? (1) Juvenal; (2) Livy; (3) Tacitus; (4) Plutarch; (5) none of the above.

18. _____ Which of the following occurred FIRST? (1) Battle of Zama; (2) Battle of Cannae; (3) destruction of Carthage; (4) Hannibal's first invasion of Italy; (5) Battle of Adrianople.

19. _____ Roman law (1) is without influence today; (2) remains a strong influence in international law and the Roman Catholic Church; (3) was almost entirely the work of the Roman Senate in the first century C.E.; (4) ignored the principle of equity; (5) is based on Salic Law.

20. _____ Cleopatra was (1) a virtuous matron of the early Republican period; (2) Nero's mother; (3) last of the Ptolemies and ruler of Egypt; (4) a Roman province in Asia; (5) Octavian's wife.

21. _____ European barbarians often attacked or migrated to Roman provinces because (1) they themselves had been attacked by Asian barbarians; (2) they were attracted by the lure of loot; (3) they were land hungry; (4) they wanted to become part of the Roman Empire; (5) all of the above.

22. _____ Each of the following was a Germanic invader of Rome EXCEPT the (1) Huns; (2) Ostrogoths; (3) Visigoths; (4) Lombards; (5) Franks.

23. _____ The *Torah* is (1) local centers of worship and instruction in the Jewish faith; (2) the title given to the patriarch of the Orthodox Church; (3) scholars in Judaic law who apply ancient Hebrew teachings to modern problems; (4) God's law as recorded by Moses as contained in the *Pentateuch*; (5) none of the above.

24. _____ Which of the following is NOT considered one of the early church officials? (1) deacon; (2) presbyter; (3) cardinal; (4) bishop; (5) archbishop.

25. _____ Which of the following occurred FIRST? (1) the birth of Jesus; (2) Pompey makes Judea a Roman province; (3) end of the Babylonian Captivity of the Jews; (4) reign of King Herod; (5) emergence of the Pharisee sect.

26. _____ Before conversion to Christianity, Saul of Tarsus was (1) a Sadducee; (2) a Pharisee; (3) an Essene; (4) a Gnostic; (5) none of the above.

27. _____ Which of the following was NOT one of the early church leaders? (1) St. Ambrose; (2) St. Jerome; (3) St. Augustine; (4) St. Anthony; (5) St. Benedict.

28. _____ Which of the following was a victim of persecution by Christians who was killed by a Christian mob in Alexandria in 415 C.E.? (1) Deborah; (2) Hypatia; (3) Livia; (4) Mary Magdalene; (5) none of the above.

29. _____ Among the early leaders of the Christian faith, Paul of Tarsus was notable for all of the following reasons EXCEPT (1) his declaration of the Petrine doctrine; (2) his assertion that Jesus was the Son of God; (3) his assertion that faith in the saving power of Jesus Christ offered salvation to Jews and non-Jews alike; (4) his successful efforts in spreading the Christian message throughout the Roman Empire; (5) his conversion to Christianity on the road to Damascus.

30. _____ The Benedictine rule of monasticism included vows to adhere to all of the following EXCEPT (1) poverty; (2) silence; (3) chastity; (4) obedience; (5) regimented schedules.

31. _____ In part, the Nicene Creed was (1) an effort to end persecution of Christians by adding pagan rituals to Christian worship; (2) a move to restore Jewish beliefs to Christian theology; (3) a hope that the barbarians would become Christians if the gospel was made available in their language; (4) an effort to combat heresy within the Christian church; (5) an attempt to bring Christians and Jews together.

32. _____ Followers of Germanic warrior leaders were known as the (1) volk; (2) salians; (3) comitatus; (4) bot; (5) none of the above.

THE PLACE

A. *On the following map, plot the boundary of the Roman Empire at its height.*

B. *Label each of the following rivers: Rhine, Nile, Elbe, Danube, and Euphrates.*

C. *With appropriate symbols and lines, show the location of each of the following on the map: Hadrian's Wall, Pontus, Gaul, and Germania. In the lower left corner of the map, include a legend explaining your lines and symbols.*

D. *Indicate the location of each of the places listed below on the map by placing the initial letter of each on the map. Be prepared to explain why each place was important in the history of Roman civilization.*

Sicily	Zama
Carthage	Macedonia
Pontus	Vesuvius
Actium	Rome

E. *Indicate by name the approximate location of the major modern nations whose territories were included in the Roman Empire at its largest extent.*

DO YOU KNOW THE SIGNIFICANCE OF THESE TERMS?

This chapter contains some terms that may be unfamiliar. Identify and state the historical significance of each to show how they represent important historical trends and tendencies.

fasces

Concilium Plebis

Code of the Twelve Tables

pater familias

Punic Wars

Marcus Aurelius

Circus Maximus

veto

Paul of Tarsus

asceticism

Alaric

Ravenna

Pantheon

Livy

Galen

RELATIONSHIPS IN TIME

A. *Each of Rome's chronological periods seems to have its own theme. The Early Period—before _____, when the Republic was established—was one of settlements and invasions. Put the following events in chronological order by numbering them.*

1. _____ Etruscan conquest of Rome

2. _____ Greek colonists arrive

3. _____ Indo-Europeans invade the Italian peninsula

4. _____ Legendary founding of Rome

5. _____ Etruscan invaders arrive

B. *During the early Republic, the dates of which were _____, Rome broadened its power to include territories all around the Mediterranean. Below is a list of events that occurred during this period, each of which increased Rome's strength outside of the Italian peninsula. Number the following items in the order of their occurrence.*

1. _____ Macedonians defeated and Greece allied with Rome

2. _____ Third Punic War

3. _____ Rome supreme in the ancient world

4. _____ Rome defeats the Latin League

5. _____ Corinth destroyed and Greece brought under direct Roman control

6. _____ First Punic War

7. _____ King of Pergamum dies, willing his country to Rome

8. _____ Second Punic War

What happened in 509 B.C.E. that led to the founding of the Republic?

Who was Rome's enemy in the Punic Wars?

What two cities did Rome demolish in 146 B.C.E., and why?

C.   *The late Republic, the dates of which were _____, was wracked by a series of civil wars between rivals within the government. Fill in the missing name in each of the pairs of opponents and number them in correct order.*

1. _____ Antony vs. _____

2. _____ Marius vs. _____

3. _____ Pompey vs. _____

In the last of the three civil wars, a woman played a key role. Who was she, and what was her importance?

D.   *The* Pax Romana *provided more than 200 years of relative peace and stability between the years _____ and _____. The rulers listed below deserve a share of the credit for the* Pax Romana; *number them in order.*

1. _____ Flavian emperors

2. _____ Augustus (Octavian)

3. _____ Antonines

4. _____ Julio-Claudian emperors

How would you briefly describe the Roman Empire during the *Pax Romana*?

E.	The rise of Christianity was one of the most important events during the era of the Roman Empire. Number each of the following events in chronological order.

1.	_____ Christianity declared official state religion

2.	_____ Execution of Jesus Christ

3.	_____ Paul of Tarsus begins spreading the Christian message

4.	_____ Edict of Milan

5.	_____ Reign of Herod the Great

COMPARING THE ROMANS WITH THE GREEKS

The Romans borrowed extensively from the Greeks. Specifically describe in what ways the Romans were similar to and different from the Greeks in the following areas.

Architecture

Sculpture

Literature

What unique contributions did the Romans make in government and law?

In temperament, attitude, and interests, how did the Romans differ from the Greeks?

ARRIVING AT CONCLUSIONS

Here are some quotations from scholars dealing with the significance of this period of history. Answer the accompanying questions briefly and be prepared to defend your position.

1.	"The slave systems of Rome and the [seventeenth-century] Iberian colonies were similar in numerous ways. They both employed a great number of slaves, and the prosperity of the elite was supported by the labor of the large slave population. They both relied on urban markets for profitable sale of the commodities produced. Yet, there were also major differences between the systems. The Roman slave system was based on food production in the heartland of the empire. The Iberian slave system rested on a foundation of luxury production, not the production of prime necessities, and it was located in the newly acquired colonial territories. . . .

"It has often been suggested that slavery retarded technological progress, a Roman weak point, by rendering labor-saving devices and techniques unnecessary. . . . To address satisfactorily the question of Roman industrial backwardness and technological stagnation requires a different perspective. . . . Owners generally lacked the specialized knowledge of the processes involved, and workers [slave or free] who might have devised labor-saving techniques or tools had no incentive or means for putting them to use." (William D. Phillips, Jr., *Slavery from Roman Times to the Early Transatlantic Trade* [Minneapolis: Univ. of Minnesota Press, 1985], pp. 12, 25.)

How did Roman slavery differ from that of other ancient or early modern societies? Do you think Roman achievements justified the use of slave labor? How significant was slavery among the economic causes of Rome's decline?

2. Representative democracy became the government of Athens during its golden age. But no democracy ever appeared in Rome. C. Northcote Parkinson offers an explanation of why it did not.

> "The main obstacle to the establishment of a democratic form of government lay in the mere size of the problem. The Athenians were relatively few and could make some pretence of assembling a representative body of citizens to conduct business on democratic lines. But the practical difficulty (and doubtful wisdom) of assembling the citizens of Rome was manifest. The eventual result could only be chaos, as the more responsible citizens could see for themselves. Even, however, if the practical problems were solved, the decisions reached would not be democratic in any real sense of the word. The vote did not extend to the rest of Italy, still less to the Roman Empire as a whole. Nor could it be extended more widely against the opposition of those already voting. The decisions made would nevertheless affect a vast and growing territory—countries which the Roman voters had never seen and could not, perhaps, have even found on the map. There was far less moral basis for a democracy in Rome than there had been for democracy in Athens. In the most careful analysis, it did not even make sense."
> (C. Northcote Parkinson, *The Evolution of Political Thought* [New York: Viking Press, 1960], pp. 183–84.)

Why do you think Parkinson regards the mass assembly of Roman citizens as a bad idea? What conditions favored democracy in Athens that did not exist in Rome? To what extent do Parkinson's strictures on democracy in ancient Rome apply to the contemporary United States?

3. "If a man were called to fix the period in the history of the world during which the condition of the human race was most happy and prosperous, he would, without hesitation, name that which elapsed from the death of Domitian to the accession of Commodus. The vast extent of the Roman empire was governed by absolute power, under the guidance of virtue and wisdom. The armies were restrained by the firm but gentle hand of four successive emperors whose characters and authority commanded involuntary respect. The forms of the civil administration were carefully preserved by Nerva, Trajan, Hadrian, and the Antonines, who delighted in the image of liberty and were pleased with considering themselves as the accountable ministers of the laws. Such princes [would have] deserved the honor of restoring the republic, had the Romans of their days been capable of enjoying a rational freedom." (Edward Gibbon, *The Decline and Fall of the Roman Empire*, abridged by D. A. Saunders [New York: The Penguin English Library, 1984], p. 107.)

Would you agree with Gibbon's opening statement? How does he insinuate in the last two sentences that Roman government, even at its best, suffered from a basic defect?

QUESTIONS TO THINK ABOUT

1. Can physical environment, more than any other factor, explain the rise of the Romans to a world power? Why or why not?

2. How does the story of the Gracchi illustrate what we call "culture lag"?

3. In what basic ways were the Romans originators and in what manner borrowers and adapters?

4. Do you think Caesar was justified in establishing a dictatorship?

5. Does Rome's achievement of cultural diversity within political unity offer any lesson for Europe?

6. Why were the Romans eager for new religions and philosophies in the fourth century? Can you see any similarity to this in our own time?

7. How did the Romans, as builders, reflect and meet the needs of a great empire?

8. What social changes occurred simultaneous with Rome's transition from republic to empire?

9. What major factors contributed to the decline of the Roman Empire in the West? Consider the economy, Christianity, and Germanic invasions in particular.

10. To what extent were the Germanic contacts with the Roman Empire invasions, and to what extent did they represent migration and assimilation?

CHAPTER 6

The Eastern Mediterranean World, 300–750 C.E.

During the period known as Late Antiquity, from the fourth century to the early part of the eighth century, the eastern Mediterranean world was changing dramatically. A new dynasty, the Sasanids, envisioned the revitalization of the Persian empire. The decline and collapse of Roman authority in the West and the relocation of the center of power and Greek and Roman culture to Byzantium resulted in a new empire in the East. In Arabia, a new religion, Islam, emerged to provide the foundation for an expansive empire. In fact, all three eastern European empires were heavily concerned with promoting religion along with the advancement of the interests of state: the Sasanids promoted Zoroastrianism, the Byzantines promoted Greek Orthodox Christianity, and Muhammad and his successors promoted Islam.

While agriculture certainly formed the base of the economy and most people still lived in small villages and towns, urban areas began to flower in the eastern Mediterranean as centers of commerce and administration. It was in this climate that the three empires with their universalist religions drew on established traditions of government, society, and culture to create an atmosphere of competition, conflict, and continued change.

YOU SHOULD HAVE A BASIC UNDERSTANDING OF:

The Eastern Mediterranean milieu.

The Sasanid Empire.

Byzantium, Constantinople, and Christianity.

Muhammad and the birth of Islam.

The Arab-Islamic Empire.

HAVE YOU MASTERED THE BASIC FACTS?

Fill in each of the following blanks with the correct identification.

The Eastern Mediterranean Milieu

1. _____: Underground water network in Iran, which is a good example of the continuing importance of agriculture in the eastern Mediterranean.

2. _____: Name given to the type of religion that advances the notion that its teachings have appeal across region, language, ethnicity, and culture, extending to all humankind.

3. _____: Syncretic faith originating in the third century, based on the teachings of the Prophet Mani, influenced by Christianity and other faiths.

The Sasanid Empire

4. _____: Ancient Persian dynasty that laid the foundation for future governments in Iran, relying on satraps as administrators in matters of state.

5. _____: Name of the founder of the dynasty that ruled Iran and adjacent regions from 224 to 651 C.E.

6. _____: Under his reign, the Sasanid Empire expanded to its greatest extent.

7. _____: Built across the Tigris from Seleucia, it was an important administrative and cultural center.

Byzantium, Constantinople, and Christianity

8. _____: Term used to refer to the Byzantine emperor's control over spiritual as well as temporal matters; the Council of Nicaea is an example.

9. _____: Sixth-century emperor who codified Roman law and began a massive building project in Constantinople. His efforts at restoring imperial control over the western part of the empire proved less successful.

10. _____: Uprising in 532 C.E. that almost drove Justinian from power.

11. _____: Empress of Justinian who was a wise counselor and courageous in times of danger.

12. _____: Greatest architectural monument of the Byzantine Empire; it proclaimed a new and lustrous civilization.

13. _____: Governing structure introduced by Heraclius in the seventh century that was designed to create a more efficient system for administrative and defense purposes.

14. _____: Ninth-century Byzantine empress who led the iconophilism movement.

15. _____: Famous map that symbolizes the continuing influence of the Greeks.

16. _____: Bitter religious conflict over the worship of images, which finally helped cause a schism between the Orthodox and Roman churches.

Muhammad and the Birth of Islam

17. _____: Located at the site of an oasis in the Hijaz region of the Arabian peninsula, this city became a major center of trade and religious worship prior to 500 C.E.

18. _____: Name for the religious beliefs of many pre-Islamic Arabs, in which gods and spirits were believed to inhabit natural objects such as stones, trees, and wells.

19. _____: Male elder who was elected to be the leader of an Arab tribe.

20. _____: Tribe that gained a prominent position in the affairs of Mecca by 500 C.E. by forging commercial relationships with Byzantium, Persia, and Aksum.

21. _____: Word meaning "submission to God."

22. _____: Holiest temple in Mecca, it contains a black stone, the most sacred relic in Arabia, supposed to have been turned black by the sins of those who touched it.

23. _____: The one god of Islam.

24. _____: Muhammad's flight from Mecca to Medina, which marked the beginning of the first year of the Muslim calendar.

25. _____: A collection of the sayings, deeds and traditions of the prophet Muhammad.

26. _____: First successor of Muhammad, he began the compilation of Muhammad's revelations into the Qur'an.

27. _____: The first four caliphs who succeeded Muhammad as head of the umma.

28. _____: Language of the Qur'an, the common knowledge of which is a force binding together present-day Muslims.

29. _____, _____, _____, _____, and _____: These are called the Five Pillars of Islam, religious acts required of every true Muslim.

The Arab-Islamic Empire

30. _____: This religious group was also a major political force beginning in the late seventh century and became an important source of anti-Umayyad activity.

31. _____: Major sect of Islam, whose members believed that the caliph owed his position to the consent of the Islamic community.

32. _____: Shrine built by the Umayyads in Jerusalem in the late seventh century near the "wailing wall," it houses a rock believed to be the site where God asked Abraham to sacrifice his son.

33. _____: Proclaimed himself caliph and founded the Umayyad dynasty in 661.

34. _____: Capital city of the Islamic Empire under the Umayyads.

TRY THESE MULTIPLE-CHOICE QUESTIONS

1. _____ Term that refers to polytheistic worship traditions: (1) Gnosticism; (2) Manichaeism; (3) Zoroastrianism; (4) Paganism; (5) none of the above.

2. _____ Which of the following was NOT a major dynasty in ancient Iran? (1) Achaemenids; (2) Pahlavis; (3) Parthians; (4) Seleucids; (5) none of the above.

3. _____ The so-called Second Rome was the city of (1) Moscow; (2) Kiev; (3) Novgorod; (4) Constantinople; (5) Ravenna.

4. _____ Justinian wasted much of the financial strength of his empire and exhausted much of its human resources in his (1) efforts to restore the western half of the Roman Empire to Constantinople's control; (2) battles to repel the Arabs; (3) campaign to take Egypt from the Muslims; (4) attempts to conquer North Africa; (5) all of the above.

5. _____ Choose the number at the end of this question that indicates the correct generalizations about the longevity of the Byzantine Empire: (a) Its command economy made it relatively immune to economic fluctuations. (b) Its sea power and advanced military technology gave it an edge over most of its opponents. (c) After losing African and western European territories, its population was culturally and linguistically relatively homogeneous. (d) Its geographic location made the capital city easily defensible. (1) a and c; (2) b and c; (3) b, c, and d; (4) only d; (5) a, b, c, and d.

6. _____ The Byzantines' defeat by Muslim Arabs at the battle of Yarmuk in 636 C.E. was significant because (1) Byzantium lost control over Jerusalem and Syria; (2) the Byzantines' defeat signaled the decline of the Byzantine empire; (3) that and subsequent victories that year allowed the Arabs to mount a direct attack on Constantinople; (4) Heraclius was forced to abdicate the throne; (5) all of the above.

7. _____ Which of the following occurred FIRST? (1) schism between eastern and western Christianity; (2) Council of Chalcedon; (3) Second Ecumenical Council; (4) end of the iconoclastic controversy; (5) reforms of Constantine V.

8. _____ Medina is a holy city for Muslims because it (1) was the birthplace of Muhammad; (2) was the home of the Ka'ba; (3) was a place of refuge for Muhammad and his followers during a time of persecution; (4) was the site of Muhammad's death; (5) all of the above.

9. _____ Which of the following occurred FIRST? (1) end of the Umayyad dynasty; (2) origin of the caliphate of Cordova; (3) the Hijra; (4) the death of Muhammad; (5) the death of Ali.

10. _____ The Shia sect differed from the Sunnis in part because it (1) opposed the use of Arabic in Muslim ritual; (2) wanted to launch a holy war against Christianity; (3) accepted a divine-right doctrine that assumed the existence of an infallible leader; (4) endorsed the Kharijites; (5) all of the above.

11. _____ The obligations Islam imposed on its followers include all of the following EXCEPT (1) poverty; (2) prayer; (3) almsgiving; (4) periodic fasting; (5) confession of faith.

12. _____ Islamic law is based primarily on (1) the Qur'an; (2) Roman law; (3) Justinian's Code; (4) Hammurabi's Code; (5) the Talmud.

13. _____ Islam expanded rapidly under the first four caliphs for all of the following reasons EXCEPT (1) its belief in Holy War (*jihad*); (2) its alliance with the Byzantines; (3) dissension among Christians; (4) the simplicity and power of its religious teachings; (5) complete unity among all Muslim groups, the umma.

14. _____ The non-Islamic populations under Muslim rule typically were (1) taxed more than Muslims; (2) subject to capital punishment; (3) excluded from the army and other public employment; (4) allowed to worship publicly and to proselytize among Muslims; (5) none of the above.

RELATIONSHIPS IN TIME

In each of the groups below, number the items in chronological order.

A. The Eastern Mediterranean Milieu; The Sasanid Empire

1. _____ Seleucid monarchy

2. _____ Arab conquest of the Sasanid Empire

3. _____ emergence of the rabbinate

4. _____ reign of Ardashir I

5. _____ appearance of Manichaeism

6. _____ construction of Ctesiphon

7. _____ reign of Alexander the Great

8. _____ reign of Shapur I

B. Byzantium, Constantinople, and Christianity

1. _____ dedication of Constantinople

2. _____ reign of Basil II

3. _____ reign of Empress Irene

4. _____ Third Ecumenical Council

5. _____ Macedonian dynasty

6. _____ iconoclasm controversy

7. _____ Madaba Mosaic

8. _____ rise of Seljuk Turks

9. _____ Great Schism

C.   **Muhammad and the Birth of Islam; The Arab-Islamic Empire**

1.   _____ rule of the first four Caliphs

2.   _____ second civil war

3.   _____ birth of Muhammad

4.   _____ Muhammad returns to Mecca

5.   _____ fall of the Umayyad dynasty

6.   _____ reign of Marwin I

7.   _____ Dome of the Rock built

8.   _____ Muslim armies take Jerusalem

9.   _____ Hijra

DO YOU KNOW THE SIGNIFICANCE OF THESE TERMS?

The following terms in this chapter represent important historical trends and tendencies. In the space provided, identify and define each of the terms and explain their significance for world history.

exilarch

Theodora

Code of Justinian

Hagia Sophia

satraps

Khusraw Anushirwan

iconoclasm

Mecca

Ka'ba

Qur'an

umma

caliph

Sunna

jihad

Dome of the Rock

THE PLACE

The Sasanid Empire; Byzantium, Constantinople, and Christianity; Islam

On the following outline map, provide the following information.

A.   *Indicate by drawing a bold, solid line the Sasanid Empire at its greatest extent.*

B.   *With a heavy pencil line, encircle the approximate area controlled by the East Roman Empire at its high point under Justinian.*

C.   *Indicate with ////// the approximate area controlled by the Muslim Arabs circa 750 C.E.*

D.   *Indicate with ------- the approximate area within the orbit of the Roman Catholic Church by 1054 C.E.*

E.   *Indicate with ===== the area within the orbit of the Eastern Orthodox Church by 1054 C.E.*

F.   *Write in the correct answer for each of the following questions, and place the number for that question at its corresponding position on the map.*

1.   _____: Site of the Second Rome

2.   _____: Location of Ctesiphon

3.   _____: Sea that separates the Italian Peninsula and the Balkans

4.   _____: Location of Mecca

5.   _____: Location of Damascus

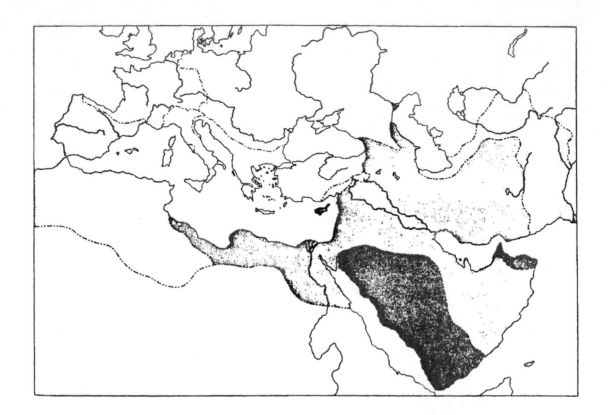

ARRIVING AT CONCLUSIONS

Here are some quotations from modern scholars dealing with the significance of this period of history. Answer the accompanying questions and be prepared to defend your position.

1. "In the late second and third centuries, the Christians became figures to be reckoned with in the Roman world. They did so largely because they had a singularly articulate and radical contribution to make to that great debate . . . on the manner in which supernatural power could be exercised in society. The way in which the Christians idealized their martyrs as the special 'friends of God,' and the manner in which they organized themselves around bishops who claimed with increasing assertiveness to be 'friends of God' . . . condensed the main issues of that debate. . . . How the Christians thought about themselves . . . and the way in which they articulated their attitude to themselves and to the outside world counted for more than spectacular or massive conversions." (Peter Brown, *The Making of Late Antiquity* [Cambridge, MA: Harvard University Press, 1978], p. 57.)

    Do you think that the author's emphasis on the power of spiritual or ideological convictions is supported by historical evidence? Do you think that it is appropriate to compare the Christian movement of late antiquity with radical movements of modern times?

2. The sixth-century Byzantine historian, Procopius, who privately condemned Emperor Justinian's character and policies, wrote for the public the following eulogy:

"In our time Justinian became Emperor. He took over the state when it was tottering dangerously. He increased its size and made it far more glorious by driving from it the barbarians who had violated it from ancient times. . . . Justinian did not refuse to acquire other states as well . . . and he built innumerable new cities. Finding doctrine about God before his time wavering and being forced into many directions, he checked all the pathways leading to error and caused the faith to stand on one secure foundation. Besides this, he found that the laws were obscure because they had been multiplied unnecessarily and were in confusion because of the obvious contradiction. So he purified them of the mass of quibbles, and by greatly strengthening them, preserved them from contradiction. The good that was done by his building shall be my present subject." Procopius then describes in detail the church of Holy Wisdom and many other great works of architecture. (Procopius, *Buildings*, trans. by Averil Cameron [New York: Twayne Publishers, 1967], pp. 333–34.)

How accurate is the above summary of Emperor Justinian's achievements? Compare it to the description in the text. What were the emperor's religious policies? Was he orthodox?

3. "The strategy employed by the Arabs in the great campaigns of conquest was determined by the use of desert power, on lines strikingly similar to the use of sea power by modern empires. The desert was familiar and accessible to the Arabs and not to their enemies. They could use it as a means of communication for supplies and reinforcements, as a safe retreat in times of emergency. It is no accident that in each of the conquered provinces the Arabs established their main bases in towns on the edge of the desert. . . . These garrison towns were the Gibraltars and Singapores of the early Arab Empire." (Bernard Lewis, *The Arabs in History* [London: Hutchinson & Co., 1960], p. 55.)

Does the analogy used by Lewis seem to be supported by his evidence? Why or why not? Does this interpretation fit the outlines of the early Arab conquests? Explain. What other factors—geographic, military, religious, and historical—were involved in the initial success of the Arabs?

4. "Perhaps . . . [an] explanation can be given for the acceptance of Arab rule by the population of the conquered territories. . . . To most of them it did not much matter whether they were ruled by Iranians, Greeks or Arabs. Government impinged for the most part on the life of the cities and their immediate hinterlands; . . . city-dwellers might not care much who ruled them, provided they were secure, at peace and reasonably taxed. The people of the countryside and steppes lived under their own customs, and it made little difference to them who ruled the cities. For some, the replacement of Greeks and Iranians by Arabs even offered advantages. Those whose opposition to Byzantine rule was expressed in terms of religious dissidence might find it easier to live under a ruler who was impartial towards various Christian groups, particularly as the new faith, which had as yet no fully developed system of doctrine or law, may not have appeared alien to them. In those parts of Syria and Iraq already occupied by people of Arabian origin and language, it was easy for their leaders to transfer their loyalties from the emperors to the new Arab alliance. . . ." (Albert Hourani, *A History of the Arab Peoples* [New York: MJF Books, 1991], pp. 23–24.)

What social, economic, and political circumstances in the Middle East during the seventh century worked in favor of the Muslim conquerors? What does Hourani suggest about the effectiveness of Byzantine and Persian rule in the Middle East? Why did some religious minorities living in the region prefer to be ruled by Muslims rather than the Byzantine emperor? Can you identify other factors that contributed to the rapid expansion of the Islamic empire?

QUESTIONS TO THINK ABOUT

1.   How did emphasis on agricultural production and trade in the area of the eastern Mediterranean contribute to the ascendancy of universalist faiths?

2.   What is meant by reference to the "preservative" functions of Byzantium? Can you think of any current cultures that may someday be remembered for a similar role?

3.   What factors do you think were most important to the rise of the Sasanids? Why? What factors might have contributed to their collapse? What were their contributions to world history? Explain your response using specific examples as illustrations.

4.   The study of history provides us with a more complete understanding of the issues and problems confronting the modern world. Can you identify any contemporary problems or conflicts that are rooted in the ambitions, actions, choices, or philosophical ideals adopted by the peoples who lived during this crucial period of history? What role did geography play in the events we have studied?

5.   Based on your reading of the "Global Issues" piece entitled "Church and State," summarize the discussion regarding how societies have managed the relationship between church and state. How is this issue approached today in different parts of the world? How are these issues relevant to today's world?

6.   What is Islam? What role has the Qu'ran played in its development, and what role does it play today?

7.   How does the role of Muhammad in the rise of Islam support the view that the personality of great individuals can determine the course of history?

CHAPTER 7

The Islamic World, 800–1300 C.E.

Islam in its early years spread with incredible rapidity across North Africa to Spain and through the Near East into Persia. This remarkable achievement was due to the attraction of Muhammad's monotheistic religious vision and the zeal of those who came after him. Both simple and profound, Islam created a community of believers, called Muslims, around the conviction that Allah is God and Muhammad is the last and greatest of his prophets. In the Qur'an, the book of Muhammad's revelations, Muslims found the guidelines for living in submission to Allah and for bringing many nations under its sway.

Muslims created a vast empire, knitted together by a common language, Arabic; the shared values of religion; and economic connections. In the period of its greatest glory, from the eighth to the twelfth centuries, Islam made major contributions to the arts and sciences and absorbed much of the culture of ancient Greece and of Persia. Although marked by internal religious and political struggles, often at war, and eventually moving toward decentralization, Islamic powers introduced a new era of cross-fertilization of Arab, Jewish, Christian, Persian, and Hellenistic traditions.

YOU SHOULD HAVE A BASIC UNDERSTANDING OF:

The early Abbasid Caliphate, 750–1000.

The shaping of Early Islamic faith and culture.

The Fatimid Empire, 909–1171.

Turkic peoples and the Islamic Near East, 1000–1200.

Resisting the Crusades.

The Islamic world, 1100–1300: unity and diversity.

HAVE YOU MASTERED THE BASIC FACTS?

Fill in each of the following blanks with the correct identification.

The Abbasid Era

1. _____: Sworn in as the first Abbasid caliph in 749 in Iraq.

2. _____: "City of Peace," its official name was Madinat; it was a new city constructed by caliph Abu Ja'far al-Mansur in the eighth century.

3. _____: The greatest Abbasid ruler, under whose leadership the Abbasid Empire reached it furthest limit.

4. _____: High-ranking member of the Abassid state, second only to the caliph.

5. _____: Garrisons established during the seventh and eighth centuries, they became centers of trade and developed into urban areas.

The Shaping of Early Islamic Faith and Culture

6. _____: Generally referring to religious scholars, this term was also applied to a broad category of persons, to include prayer leaders and others who demonstrated religious knowledge.

7. _____: This term refers to those who believe that rightful leadership of the Islamic community came from male descendants of the prophet, specifically from Abi Talib and his wife Fatima (Muhammad's daughter).

8. _____: "The Mahdi," who will return to bring justice to the world some day and take vengeance on "the enemies of God."

9. _____: The largest division within Islam; this form of Islam accepts the legitimacy of the first three caliphs and believes that the caliph's authority comes from the consent of the Islamic community.

10. _____: Islamic law; it is literally the "right path" or "way" provided by divine guidance of the Qur'an and Sunna.

11. _____: A broad movement in early Islam mixing asceticism, spirituality, and the search for ultimate truths; Islamic mysticism.

12. _____: "Struggle" in Arabic; it can refer to a personal struggle to overcome sin, a struggle for social change, or a holy war.

13. _____: A Iranian scholar, mathematician, and resident of Baghdad, he wrote *The Book of Calculation Through Completion and Balancing*; from its Arabic title we get the term *algebra*.

14. _____: Eleventh-century Muslim scholar; author of the *Canon of Medicine*, also known as Avicenna.

The Fatimid Empire, 909–1171

15. _____: Palace center in Egypt named al-Qahira ("the Victorious") by the Fatimids.

16. _____: The Fatimid Empire reached its greatest extent under this ruler, who reigned during the years 975–996.

17. _____: Followers of al-Hakim, they moved to the mountains of Lebanon and are a distinct religious sect today in Lebanon, Syria, and Israel.

Turkic Peoples and the Islamic Near East, 1000–1200; Islamic Spain; Resisting the Latin Crusades; The Islamic World, 1100–1300: Unity and Diversity

18. _____: Group of Turks who gained control over Persia, Iraq, Syria, and Palestine in the eleventh century; they allowed the Abbasids to remain in power in name only.

19. _____: Islamic religious and legal academies encouraged by the Seljuq vizir Nisam al-Mulk, they became an important element of Sunni religious and cultural life throughout the Near East.

20. _____: Straits that separate North Africa and Spain, named after Tariq ibn Ziyad, an Arab commander.

21. _____: During his reign as *amir* (756–788), he unified Spain through careful administration and sharp sensitivity to its ethnic complexity.

22. _____, _____, and _____: Three caliphates that represented three distinct regions in the Islamic world by the tenth century.

23. _____: Campaigns by Catholic forces in medieval Spain to recapture territories held by Muslim states.

24. _____: Series of formal campaigns organized in medieval Europe to gain control of Jerusalem and surrounding territories from Muslim control.

25. _____: Kurdish military commander who achieved lasting fame throughout the Islamic world, from the Ayyubid dynasty, he would unify Egypt with Syria; he retook Jerusalem from the Christians but allowed Christian pilgrims access to holy sites.

26. _____: "One who is owned"; these slave soldiers established a prosperous regime in Egypt.

TRY THESE MULTIPLE-CHOICE QUESTIONS

1. _____ Literally meaning "God's deputy," it refers to the religious and political leader of the Islamic nation: (1) vizer; (2) sultan; (3) diwan; (4) caliph; (5) none of the above.

2. _____ Report or reports of the words and deeds of the Prophet; major source of guidance and rules for Islamic law: (1) *salat*; (2) umma; (3) *ulama*; (4) Hajj; (5) hadith.

3. _____ Which of the following occurred FIRST? (1) end of the Umayyad dynasty in the Near East; (2) Islamic control of Cordoba; (3) Fatimid dynasty founded; (4) Mongols sack Baghdad; (5) the First Crusade.

4. _____ Which of the following persons was NOT a major intellectual figure during the early Abbasid period? (1) Abu Tammam; (2) Ibn al-Muqaffa; 3) Ya'qub ibn Killis; (4) al-Baladhuri; (5) Abu Bakr al-Razi.

5. _____ Islamic society is typified by: (1) equality between the sexes; (2) a priestly caste; (3) separation of church and state; (4) unanimous agreement about dynastic succession; (5) none of the above.

6. _____ Islamic culture under the Abbasid dynasty reached an unparalleled level of creativity and accomplishment because (1) the Abbasid caliphs encouraged scholarship and artistic expression; (2) the Abbasid caliphs succeeded in expelling Christian and Jewish influences from their realm; (3) the Abbasid caliphs created a self-reliant economy that isolated the Islamic umma from the outside world; (4) the Abbasid caliphs successfully worked out a definitive solution to the issue of succession to the caliphate; (5) none of the above.

7. _____ The Seljuqs were (1) members of a heretical sect within Islam; (2) Turkish nomads from central Asia; (3) renegade Byzantine soldiers; (4) nomadic peoples who converted to Christianity; (5) none of the above.

8. _____ The Mamluks were (1) Muslim holy men; (2) founders of a Muslim dynasty in Spain; (3) Asian nomads who captured the city of Baghdad; (4) Jews forced out of Spain by the Moors; (5) none of the above.

9. _____ Which of the following happened LAST? (1) Seljuqs defeat Byzantines at Manzikert; (2) Mamluk kingdom established in Egypt; (3) Umayyads set up new dynasty in Spain; (4) Salah al-Din defeats crusaders and retakes Jerusalem; (5) fall of last Crusader kingdom in the Near East.

10. _____ Located in Spain, it is a magnificent example of Islamic achievement in architecture: (1) Bou Inaniya Madrasa; (2) the Alhambra; (3) Great Mosque at Samarra; (4) palace at al-Qat'i; (5) the Al-Andalus Bridge.

RELATIONSHIPS IN TIME

To give yourself a framework for understanding the development of Islam, place each of these items in its correct position on the following time line.

Ibn Sina (Avicenna)   Seljuk Turks capture Baghdad
Reign of Harun al-Rashid   Rhazes's treatises on medical science
Ibn-Khaldun   Mongols invade Persia and Iraq
Muhammad   Ibn Rushd (Averroës)
Fall of the Abbasids   Umayyads replaced by the Abbasids
First four caliphs (Rahidun)   Martyrdom of Husayn at Karbala
Muawiya   Salah al-Din
Muslims under Tariq ibn Ziyad conquer Spain

500

600

700

800

900

1000

1100

1200

1300

1400

DO YOU KNOW THE SIGNIFICANCE OF THESE TERMS?

Regarding this chapter about Islam, the following terms represent major historical developments. In the space provided, write your definition of each of the following and record your evaluation of the terms as symbols of historical significance for world history.

Abassid dynasty

Ibn Sina

Fatima

kuttab

Khurasani

Isma'ili Shi'ites

Twelver Shi'ism

dhikr

Arabic numerals

Sharia

Seljuq Turks

algebra

Map of Al-Idrisi

astrolabe

Alhambra

THE PLACE

A.   *On the following outline map, indicate with ////// the area under the control of the Abbasid dynasty.*

B.   *On the same map, indicate the location of the following places:*

      1.   Mecca
      2.   Jerusalem
      3.   Constantinople
      4.   Baghdad
      5.   Cordova
      6.   Damascus
      7.   Medina
      8.   Cairo

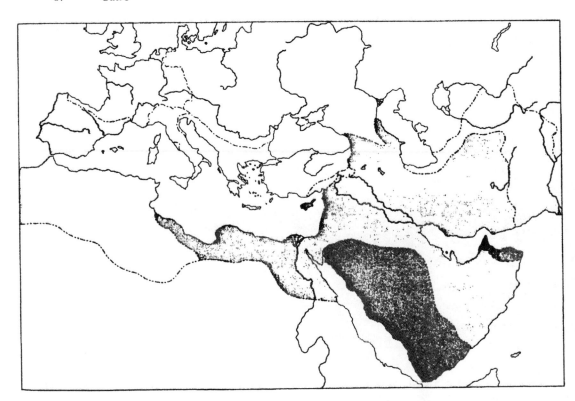

ARRIVING AT CONCLUSIONS

Here is a quotation from historians dealing with the significance of this period of history. Answer the accompanying questions briefly and be prepared to defend your position.

> "Unquestionably Allah's commands in the [Qur'an] raised the status of women in seventh-century Arabia. . . . It is true that [it] says . . . that the man is the head of the household—something that has hardly been disputed in any civilized society until the present day. It was the scholars and casuists of Islam in later centuries who succeeded in . . . misinterpreting the [Qur'an] in such a way as to place women in subjection. Seclusion and the veil which were intended to give women privacy and protection . . . became a form of imprisonment. . . . Divorce, which the [Qur'an] commands should only be practiced in exceptional circumstances, . . . became a powerful instrument of male tyranny." (Peter Mansfield, *The Arabs* [New York: Viking Penguin, 1985], p. 26.)

How does the Qur'an's treatment of women, as described by Mansfield, compare with the position of women in ancient Greek and Roman society? Why has "civilized society" always assumed that the man is the head of the household? Have you noticed signs that this idea is being challenged within Islam, as well as within other ancient civilizations?

QUESTIONS TO THINK ABOUT

1. What is Islam? What role has the Qu'ran played in its development, and what role does it play today?

2. What are some of the reasons why Muslims have divided so intensely since the Prophet's death? How have these divisions affected the areas in the world that have predominantly Muslim populations?

3. What political, economic, and social conditions help to account for the remarkable achievements in science, literature, and the arts under the Umayyad and Abbasid dynasties?

4. Compare the aspirations of Islamic fundamentalism at the end of the twentieth century with the original teachings and example of Muhammad. How do you think Muhammad would judge a regime like contemporary Iran's?

5. What has been the historical impact of the concept of the umma? In your opinion, does the term *jihad* mean "struggle" or "holy war"? Explain your answers.

6. How would you summarize the contributions of the Islamic powers to world history in terms of economic, political, and cultural aspects?

CHAPTER 8

African Beginnings:
African Civilizations to 1500 C.E.

The history of Africa ranges from the emergence of human ancestors to the development of complex societies, kingdoms, and modern states. Great diversity characterizes the continent of Africa in terms of its geography and its people as well at economic, social, cultural, and political patterns. The study of Africa is particularly interesting and challenging at the same time as much of the past has been preserved through oral tradition and much of it has been distorted or denied by colonial intrusions. But historians in the twenty-first century continue to uncover the fascinating history of Africa's past.

Life among the Bantu-speaking people was in harmony with nature's rhythms, and Africa's early empires generally developed along a course that mirrored the cultural values of their founding peoples. African societies were shaped by centuries of cultural experience in adapting to and surviving in an often difficult natural environment; and, over time, many of these societies were influenced by outside cultural forces—with both positive and negative results.

Throughout the centuries, Africans developed societies that were complex organizations that achieved high levels of skill in agriculture, architecture, crafts, engineering, and government. They also developed effective systems of social morality, prizing communal qualities rather than competition. In the process, Africans have demonstrated remarkable genius for adaptation, innovation, and ingenuity, resulting in a rich tapestry of civilizations.

YOU SHOULD HAVE A BASIC UNDERSTANDING OF:

The broad outlines of African history—its geographic, trade, ethnic, and historical background and general cultural patterns.

The civilizations of sub-Saharan Africa.

The major empires of East Africa and the Sudan.

The cross-cultural impact of the trans-Saharan and Indian Ocean trade.

Kingdoms of Central and Southern Africa.

HAVE YOU MASTERED THE BASIC FACTS?

Fill in each of the following blanks with the correct identification.

The African Environment

1. _____: Huge desert that stretches across Africa just south of the fertile strip along the north coast.

2. _____: Grassy plains that become more and more wooded as they near the equator.

3. _____: Farming method common in sparsely populated regions with marginal soil in which farmers clear a patch of land to be used for cultivation for only a few growing seasons.

4. _____ : Technique used to make bronze statuary using a wax cast and a clay mold.

5. _____ : Principle that is fundamental to social organization throughout sub-Saharan Africa.

The Peopling of Africa; Bantu Dispersion

6. _____ : Phase from 10,000 to 6,000 B.C.E. during which the northern half of Africa received abundant rainfall that supported human habitation in regions such as the Sahara Desert.

7. _____ : Dating between 700 to 400 B.C.E., this early center of iron-smelting on the Jos plateau in central Nigeria produced steel of equal quality to the iron works of Rome and Egypt.

8. _____ : Capital city of Kush and a famous iron-smelting center.

9. _____ : Language group of many eastern, central, and southern African societies that can be traced to the Bantu peoples who began migrating from their original homeland near present-day Cameroon around 500 B.C.E.

Ethiopia and Northeastern Africa

10. _____ : Fifteenth-century emperor of Ethiopia who reformed the church, strengthened the unity of the state, and achieved security among the country's Islamic neighbors.

11. _____ : Native title of the emperor of Ethiopia.

12. _____ : Bean, originally chewed as a stimulant, which could also be used to make a drink, which originated in Ethiopia and rapidly spread to Arab culture; the Arab word for it is *oahwa*.

13. _____ : Fourth-century ruler of Aksum who converted to Christianity and made it the official state religion.

14. _____ : Carved from solid rock, they became sites of pilgrammages by Christians; interior designs drew on Byzantine, Greek, and Roman motifs.

15. _____ : The royal chronicle of the Solomonid Dynasty, who succeeded the Zagwes in 1270 C.E.; it provided an epic account that claimed direct decent from the Old Testament's King Solomon.

16. _____ : According to Ethiopian church officials, the Ark of the Covenant is stored here.

17. _____ : The Ethiopian monarchy was at an apex during his reign; he sat behind a curtain when he held audience in court and forbade his subjects to look at him.

Empires of the Sudan

18. _____ : One of the kingdoms of the western Sudan, its king was considered divine, an impression reinforced when he appeared surrounded by gold swords and horses wearing gold cloth blankets.

19. _____: Most significant foreign religious influence on the kingdoms of western Sudan.

20. _____: King of Mali who dazzled Mecca with his lavish retinue and generous gifts.

21. _____: King of Songhai who organized the government to run peacefully and effectively.

22. _____: Songhai city renowned as a center of learning and trade; site of the Sankore mosque.

23. _____: Thirteenth-century king of Kanem; he amassed an impressive cavalry force that numbered as many as 40,000 horsemen.

24. _____: Pack animals that served as the primary means of transporting goods in the trans-Saharan trade.

25. _____, _____, and _____: In central Sudan, the most important of the Muslim states that emerged to take advantage of fertile agricultural lands and trans-Saharan trade routes.

Swahili City-States in East Africa

26. _____: Independent and competitive coastal centers of trade in East Africa, ruled by Muslim urban elites, whose remarkable civilization peaked between 1200 and 1500 C.E.

27. _____: Principle East African port city in the Indian Ocean trade.

28. _____: Title adopted by many Muslim monarchs of East African city-states.

29. _____: Swahili city-state that became prosperous mainly because it established control over Zimbabwe's gold exports.

30. _____: Chinese admiral who visited Swahili towns in the early 1400s.

Kingdoms of Central and Southern Africa

31. _____: Kingdom formed in the fourteenth century by Wene.

32. _____: Royal palace built by the rulers of Great Zimbabwe, it had walls twelve feet thick and twenty feet high and was more than 800 feet in circumference.

33. _____: According to traditional accounts, he was sent by the rulers of Great Zimbabwe to find new sources of salt, but eventually founded the rival kingdom of Mutapa in the Mazoe valley.

TRY THESE MULTIPLE-CHOICE QUESTIONS

1. _____ Africa's geography consists of bands of (1) large tropical rain forests which contain very fertile soil; (2) rocky coasts and desert; (3) mountainous coasts and desert in the interior; (4) fertile coasts, tropical jungles, and savanna; (5) numerous major river systems that crisscross the continent east to west.

2. _____ The accomplishments of prehistoric Africa are evident in all of these EXCEPT (1) Nok terra-cotta sculpture; (2) brass pots; (3) cultivation of sorghum; (4) the widespread use of iron; (5) pastoralism.

3. _____ Gold and salt were exchanged for centuries in the trade that crossed the (1) Niger River; (2) Indian Ocean; (3) Sahara Desert; (4) Red Sea; (5) Kalahari Desert.

4. _____ The three states that rose in the western savanna were (1) Ghana, Kush, Benin; (2) Aksum, Kush, Mali; (3) Songhai, Kongo, Mali; (4) Ghana, Mali, Songhai; (5) Zimbabwe, Kongo, Benin.

5. _____ In East Africa (1) the political units were coastal cities, not states; (2) trade in the Indian Ocean was the economic cornerstone of the culture; (3) the level of civilization was advanced; (4) monsoon winds have played important roles in promoting trade with the Near East, India and Asia; (5) all of the above.

6. _____ Zimbabwe thrived because of its (1) iron refining; (2) salt trade; (3) gold mining; (4) slave trade; (5) cotton cultivation.

7. _____ Askia Muhammed was the enlightened early sixteenth-century ruler of (1) Songhai; (2) Mali; (3) Ethiopia; (4) Kush; (5) Kilwa.

8. _____ The value system common to the Bantu-speaking people of sub-Saharan Africa included all of the following EXCEPT (1) appreciation for the interests of the community; (2) emphasis on the individual; (3) belief in a supreme being; (4) respect for the dead; (5) infanticide.

9. _____ The native cultures in Africa (1) varied greatly; (2) depended on clans for their political structure; (3) accepted the arts as an integral part of their daily lives; (4) were engaged in different types of economic activities; (5) all of the above.

10. _____ In the parts of Africa where Bantu political institutions prevailed, (1) descent in royal lines was quite commonly patrilineal; (2) women were often powers behind the thrones; (3) occasionally women served as officials or councilors; (4) a variety of political systems was used; (5) all of the above.

11. _____ Slaves in Africa (1) were an important part of the trans-Saharan trade; (2) were found in all sub-Saharan societies; (3) were considered property for life; (4) served as warriors, administrators, and diplomats; (5) all of the above.

12. _____ By the fifteenth century, the kings of Kongo had developed a centralized state including all of the following EXCEPT (1) a professional army; (2) a democratic system for selecting kings; (3) control over inter-regional trade; (4) a governing administration usually staffed by the king's relatives; (5) a functioning bureaucracy.

13. _____ *The Periplus of the Erythrean Sea* (1) described the trade network along the Red Sea and Indian Ocean; (2) was written around the first century C.E.; (3) was a navigational guide identifying the principle ports and market towns in East Africa; (4) was written by a Greek trader in Alexandria, Egypt; (5) all of the above.

14. _____ The Swahili city-states (1) were dominated by Muslim traders who formed the political elite; (2) were often dominated by the more powerful kingdoms of Ethiopia and Ghana; (3) created a centralized federation of states under a single monarch to regulate commercial competition; (4) eventually absorbed the kingdoms of Great Zimbabwe and Benin; (5) eventually formed the nation of Kenya.

15. _____ Christianity in Ethiopia was promoted by all of the following EXCEPT (1) Coptic church leaders in Egypt; (2) Syrian monks known as the "Nine Saints"; (3) leaders of the church were chosen by church councils in Ethiopia; (4) Emperor Zar'a Yakob; (5) Frumentius and Aedisius.

16. _____ All of the following were key components in the trans-Saharan trade EXCEPT (1) gold; (2) cotton; (3) kola nuts; (4) salt; (5) cloth.

17. _____ The trans-Saharan slave trade was fueled primarily by the high market demand for new sources of labor and soldiers in (1) Northern Europe; (2) the Americas; (3) Byzantium; (4) the North African Mediterranean states; (5) India.

18. _____ This city was a very important center of commerce and education in Mali and later in Songhai: (1) Aksum; (2) Mogadishu; (3) Timbuktu; (4) Zazzau; (5) Zimbabwe.

19. _____ Which of the following correctly identifies the agricultural practice of growing plants that compliment each other side by side in order to make the most use out of poor soil? (1) slash and burn; (2) bush fallow; (3) intercropping; (4) terra cotta; (5) terracing.

20. _____ Sunni Ali and Askia Muhammad were important kings who ruled during the fifteenth and sixteenth centuries over which of the following empires? (1) Songhai; (2) Aksum; (3) Benin; (4) Mapungabwe; (5) Kongo.

DO YOU KNOW THE SIGNIFICANCE OF THESE TERMS?

This chapter contains some terms that may be unfamiliar. Write a short definition of each, using the text and the dictionary when necessary and, in the space provided, explain how each of them is important for world history.

oral tradition

caravan trade

bridewealth

"stateless" societies

pastoralism

Bantu

Aksum

Jenne-jeno

Ghana

Catalan Atlas

Timbuktu

Queen Amina

Benin

Swahili states

Great Zimbabwe

FOCUSING ON MAJOR TOPICS

Fill in the blanks in the following narrative.

The most prominent of the sub-Saharan peoples were the (1) _____, who originated in the (2) _____ part of Africa. Already by 2000 B.C.E., (3) _____ and (4) _____ were being cultivated in the savanna. Beautiful terra-cotta sculpture was being fashioned by the (5) _____ people for centuries after 1000 B.C.E. The use of (6) _____ spread over much of Africa between 600 B.C.E. and 400 C.E.

The Nubian kingdom of (7) _____ emerged by the fourth century B.C.E. Its capital was (8) _____, a civilized city that traded heavily in (9) _____ tools and weapons. A hybrid Arab-African state, (10) _____, conquered Kush and took over much of the trade between Africa and the Near East. Under the fifteenth-century emperor (11) _____, the Ethiopian monarchy reached its greatest strength, but within a century a holy war launched by the Muslim state of (12) _____ brought about the decline of Aksum's power.

The three prominent kingdoms of the western Sudan between roughly 400 and 1600 were, in chronological order, (13) _____, (14) _____, and (15) _____. These kingdoms grew up around the trade crossing the (16) _____ Desert, carrying the gold that was mined near the (17) _____ River. The kingdoms sometimes had highly developed governmental systems, in spite of the fact that boundaries were fluid and cultural unity was lacking.

In East Africa, trade was concentrated along the (18) _____ from the beginning of the Common Era. After the twelfth century, the primitive trading settlements became flourishing (19) _____ commercial centers. By the fourteenth century, the commercial traffic had increased greatly in the sophisticated coastal towns, such as Kilwa. East Africa centered on a series of independent coastal (20) _____. The spoken language was (21) _____, but the literature was written in an (22) _____ script. The official religion was (23) _____, shaped by local customs and traditional beliefs.

THE PLACE

Using the maps in your textbook, locate and mark the items below on the following outline map of Africa.

Sahara Desert	Red Sea	Nile River
Cairo	Songhai	Benin
Kalahari Desert	Indian Ocean	Niger River
Mali	Zimbabwe	Kongo
Mediterranean Sea	Atlantic Ocean	Aksum
Ghana	Timbuktu	Ethiopia

ARRIVING AT CONCLUSIONS

Here are some quotations from scholars dealing with the significance of this period of history. Answer the accompanying questions briefly, and be prepared to defend your position.

1. "In summary, the social and political organization of all the Negro kingdoms had numerous features in common. . . . All . . . were highly autocratic, with power of life or death vested in the king. He also represented the court of last appeal in legal cases, and one of his important functions was dispensing justice. While benevolence in a king was appreciated, he was likely to be regarded as a weakling if he never utilized his powers arbitrarily. The person of the king was always sacred, and his physical condition was thought to affect the well-being of the state. . . . The royal establishment was always elaborate and absorbed much of the national revenue. It included guards, an elaborate cadre of court officials, and hundreds of wives. . . . None of the Negro kingdoms had legislative bodies or any other device for popular representation in government. Although the king usually had a council, the members were appointed by him, and their duties were purely advisory." (Ralph Linton, *The Tree of Culture* [New York: Alfred A. Knopf, 1955], p. 463.)

Does this seem an accurate description of the native kingdoms of Africa? Cite evidence to back up your opinion. If Linton's observations are true, what effect may these long-established cultural patterns have on the developing African nations of today? Is it likely that they will become democratic?

2. "A distinguished historian has written 'civilization is born of numbers.' Without these 'numbers,' the emperors of Ghana would never have been able to build the great palaces of Koumbi. . . . The continent was therefore densely populated, especially south of the Sahara: in the Senegal valley, in the interior of the Niger delta and around Lake Chad there were hundreds of farming villages, trading centres and towns. . . . The great monuments were not the work of 'hordes of slaves'; it was the piety of the subjects and their concept of royalty—which made each think of himself as the son of the king—that made possible these major endeavours. The coercion of 'hordes of slaves' appears more and more a superficial explanation, just as if we tried to explain a Gothic cathedral or a Roman basilica as the product of slaves working under the whip. Faith has strong echoes in the hearts and spirits of men." (D. T. Niane, ed., *Africa from the Twelfth to the Sixteenth Century* [Berkeley: University of California Press, 1984], p. 683.)

Do you agree with the author's inference that the great monuments of African civilization were truly communal endeavors comparable to the collective motivation that produced the great medieval cathedrals? What other aspects of African life had a communal rather than an individual character? Is there a connection between Africa's communal traditions and the socialist tendencies of modern African nationalist movements?

QUESTIONS TO THINK ABOUT

1. What similarities and what differences do you find between the civilizations of sub-Saharan Africa and those of North Africa before 1500?

2. Which of the sub-Saharan African civilizations we have studied do you consider particularly interesting? Explain your answer.

3. In what ways did the trans-Saharan and Indian Ocean trade have an impact on the peoples involved that went beyond national commercial relationships? In what ways did the trade affect cultural patterns?

4.   Consider the economic and political development of major areas of Africa discussed in this chapter. What are their similarities and differences? Explain your answer.

5.   Can you identify any common themes in the cultural developments of the African societies we have studied? What role did the natural environment play in the histories of African societies? To what extent were talented rulers able to shape the future of their nations?

CHAPTER 9

The Formation of Christian Europe
476–1300 C.E.

The decline and fall of the western half of the Roman Empire in the fifth century created a vacuum in Europe that was filled largely by the Roman Catholic Church and Germanic kingdoms. Rome's centralized administration, standing professional army, and uniform imperial legal system were replaced by Germanic tribal institutions or by locally adapted remnants of the Roman past. From these roots, in response to external challenges and internal needs, emerged a new economic, political-military system—feudalism—which distributed authority through a hierarchy of personal relationships between lords and vassals. Europe thus entered the medieval era, the period between the fall of Rome and the "modern" world of the Renaissance.

As a cultural force, the Church centered at Rome became the major religious and intellectual influence shaping western Europe. Among the many German tribes that invaded the empire, the Franks proved to be most politically astute and most powerful. Both qualities were exemplified in Clovis and Charlemagne, who linked their extraordinary political ambitions to the dominant religious force in western Europe, Catholic Christianity. From this union, a semblance of imperial unity among European peoples evolved—an attempt to found a Holy Roman Empire—only to develop into feudalism with the decline, albeit temporary, of both church and state.

Beginning in the eleventh century and extending through the thirteenth century, Europe underwent a period of renewal and reform. The previous era characterized by feudalism, with its decentralization of power in the economy and the state, gave way to a resurgence of secular interest. As the ideal of a united Christian Europe declined, a new ideal gradually took its place. Europe was increasingly viewed as a network of independent, sovereign states competing more than cooperating with one another. It was apparent that distinct nations were developing. In England and France, nation and state had become virtually inseparable under native ruling families or dynasties. Elsewhere, as on the Iberian peninsula, the nation-state was also coming to be the basic form of political organization. In Germany, the concept of a "holy empire" in the tradition of Rome continued but resulted in a proliferation of provinces, while the Byzantine Empire peaked and then declined. In eastern Europe, Russia, and the Slavic regions, efforts concentrated on developing national identity. Still, however, Christianity, be it Roman Catholic or Greek Orthodox, played a crucial role in the development of Europe.

In addition, the culture changed dramatically; particularly the Church changed, as it sought to reform itself in a variety of ways, internally and externally, and tried to rid the Holy Lands of the Muslims in the Crusades. Meanwhile, contact with other parts of the world, particularly connecting along the Mediterranean, resulted in stimulated trade, the rise of towns and the development of guilds, great monuments of architecture, and the foundation of universities; a new culture was in the making, a culture shaped by Germanic and Christian influences, one that seemed destined to have a broad impact on world history.

YOU SHOULD HAVE A BASIC UNDERSTANDING OF:

The evolution of the Christian Church and its presence in Europe in the Early Middle Ages.

The Merovingians and Carolingians.

The structure of feudalism, to include manorialism, and how it filled the vacuum left by the disintegration of the Carolingian Empire and the Viking invasions.

The revival of trade and towns and the rise of guilds.

Renewal of the Catholic Church during 1000–1300, as demonstrated by papal reform, formation of new orders, and the Crusades.

The development of European states, 1000–1300.

Byzantium in its Golden Age and decline.

Russia and the nations of southeastern Europe.

HAVE YOU MASTERED THE BASIC FACTS?

Fill in each of the following blanks with the correct identification.

The Catholic Church in the Early Middle Ages

1. _____: Pope who led the movement in the late sixth and early seventh centuries to use political as well as spiritual influence.

2. _____: A large grant of territory in Italy given by the Germanic ruler created the Papal States and increased the Pope's power.

3. _____: Early Christian missionary who lived with the Visigoths and translated most of the Bible into Gothic.

4. _____: Sixth-century church scholar who wrote *The Consolation of Philosophy*, a leader in the effort to preserve classical texts.

5. _____: This book stands as an outstanding example of early medieval European monastic scholarly and artistic achievement.

The Merovingians and Carolingians

6. _____: Germanic people who migrated into Gaul and built the most enduring Germanic state—this kingdom covered most of France by the early sixth century.

7. _____: Dynasty in France whose conversion to Christianity assured the support of the native population in the sixth century.

8. _____: Named not for its founder, but for the leader under whose rule the dynasty reached its height of power.

9. _____: Christian heresy rejected by Clovis in favor of orthodox, Trinitarian Christianity.

10. _____: Sea-faring Scandinavian invaders who attacked Europe from the ninth to the eleventh centuries.

Feudalism, Manorialism, and Life in the Middle Ages

11. _____: Noble who had knelt before his overlord and promised personal loyalty to him; in return he was given control over a portion of the lord's land.

12. _____: Hereditary allotment of land that the above noble received control of, but not ownership of, after his oath of fealty to his overlord.

13. _____: Lowest ranking member of the feudal nobility.

14. _____: Process by which vassals parceled out portions of their fiefs to lesser members of the nobility.

15. _____: Manorial land reserved exclusively for the lord's use.

16. _____: Hereditary servile class bound to manorial land in the feudal system.

17. _____: Most leaders of the Church came from this social class.

18. _____: It was a code of conduct traditionally based on warfare, religion, and reverence to women and formed the basis for medieval European culture.

19. _____: The highpoint of the ceremony emphasizing a newly designated knight's responsibilities.

20. _____: A ruler or state that exercises control over another individual or state.

21. _____: On the feudal manor, the part of the land reserved for the feudal lord's use alone.

22. _____, _____: The most popular pastimes of medieval peasants included these activities.

The Revival of Trade and Towns

23. _____: Class of workers in a craft guild who had completed the initial stage of training in their trade but had not yet produced a "master piece."

24. _____: Determined by the guild to be fair to both producer and consumer, this term refers to what the customer paid for goods.

25. _____: Association of artisans or merchants formed to meet business, political, and social objectives.

The Church in the High Middle Ages: 1000–1348

26. _____: Order of friars who rejected riches and emphasized a spiritual message of poverty and Christian simplicity.

27. _____: Lawyer pope under whose administration the papacy reached a high point in power.

28. _____ : Belief in teachings condemned by the Church.

29. _____ : Series of military expeditions from western Europe aimed at removing Muslim control of the Holy Lands.

The Development of European States: 1000–1348

30. _____ : French king who accomplished the first great expansion of territory, tripling the monarchy's holdings.

31. _____ : English ruler best known for increasing the power of the royal courts at the expense of the feudal courts.

32. _____ : Archbishop of Canterbury who defied Henry II and became a martyr to protect church courts.

33. _____ : Movement in Spain characterized by religious fervor directed at removal of the Muslims.

Byzantium in Its Golden Age and Decline

34. _____ : Dynasty during whose time (867–1056) the Byzantine Empire enjoyed political and cultural superiority over its foes.

35. _____ : Alphabet of modified Greek characters adapted to the Slavic languages.

36. _____ : Female historian, author of numerous works, including *The Alexiad.*

Russia and the Nations of Southeastern Europe

37. _____ : Son of the diplomatically astute prince of Novgorod, Alexander Nevsky, who founded the Grand Duchy of Moscow.

38. _____ : Asian invaders who conquered Russia and imposed political control between 1240 and 1480 C.E.

39. _____ : The ruler of the Kiev Rus' who brought his country into the Byzantine sphere by marrying the sister of the Byzantine emperor and by officially embracing the Orthodox faith.

40. _____ : People from northern Europe who established political control over Kiev and Novgorod during the ninth and tenth centuries under Oleg and Sviatoslav.

41. _____ : This battle in Serbia in 1389 brought the collapse of Slavic political cohesiveness at the hands of the Ottoman Turks.

42. _____ : Area in Slavic Europe, under Roman control for almost 200 years; became highly Latinized.

TRY THESE MULTIPLE-CHOICE QUESTIONS

1. _____ One of the greatest Catholic missionaries to the Germanic tribes, known as "Apostle to the Germans," was (1) Gregory I; (2) Cassiodorus; (3) Boethius; (4) Boniface; (5) Augustine.

2. _____ As monasteries became the repositories of classical learning, many of them established special departments to copy manuscripts—departments known as (1) abbeys; (2) scriptoria; (3) marches; (4) bishoprics; (5) rectories.

3. _____ The Merovingian ruler whose conquests in the late fifth and early sixth centuries brought most of France under Frankish control was (1) Charles Martel; (2) Einhard; (3) Syagrius; (4) Clovis I; (5) Louis the Pious.

4. _____ The alliance between the papacy and the Frankish state had lasting significance on the history of western Europe because (1) the pope was forced to accept the status of vassal under the Frankish king; (2) the Frankish king was able to absorb all papal lands and unite the Italian peninsula; (3) the Franks replaced the Byzantines as the protector of the Roman church; (4) Charlemagne used the church to legitimize his military conquest of Britain; (5) all of the above.

5. _____ The adversaries at the battle of Tours in 732 were the (1) Franks and Muslims; (2) Lombards and Slavs; (3) Byzantines and Muslims; (4) Lombards and Byzantines; (5) Capetians and Normans.

6. _____ Which of the following occurred FIRST? (1) Battle of Tours; (2) Charles Martel became mayor; (3) Pepin the Short became mayor; (4) Charlemagne was crowned emperor; (5) Vikings raided England.

7. _____ Charlemagne's capital, which he called New Rome, was located at (1) Tours; (2) Aix-la-Chapelle; (3) Poiters; (4) Paris; (5) Seville.

8. _____ Feudalism has as a major characteristic (1) the utilization of machinery to stimulate industrial production; (2) the decentralization of political authority; (3) efforts to eliminate violence and war; (4) rejection of Christianity; (5) all of the above.

9. _____ A basic feature of the feudal system is (1) the association of land ownership and military power; (2) the strict separation of church and state; (3) participation in government by all classes; (4) rapid social and political change; (5) strict division of labor for peasants, based on gender.

10. _____ One of the ways by which the Church attempted to exercise control of knights was by urging knights to protect sacred places and spare noncombatants, a pronouncement known as (1) the Penitence of Warriors; (2) the Truce of God; (3) the Peace of God; (4) the Code of Chivalry; (5) none of the above.

11. _____ Nobles were fond of participating in all of the following outdoor sports as entertainment EXCEPT: (1) jousting; (2) cockfighting; (3) falconry; (4) hunting; (5) fighting with quarterstaves.

12. _____ In the manorial system, the person who was the general manager of the lord's estate was the (1) steward; (2) bailiff; (3) reeve; (4) freeman; (5) maitre d'.

13. _____ The battle of Hastings was won by the (1) Saxons; (2) Normans; (3) Slavs; (4) Magyars; (5) Anglos.

14. _____ William the Conqueror introduced feudalism to England, (1) requiring all vassals to swear their first allegiance to the king, rather than to another vassal; (2) requiring tenants-in-chief to provide knights for the royal army; (3) retaining some land for his royal domain; (4) all of the above; (5) none of the above.

15. _____ Henry II and Thomas à Becket quarreled over (1) Henry's desire for a divorce; (2) the independence of church courts; (3) Becket's affair with Henry's wife; (4) the practice of investiture; (5) all of the above.

16. _____ Among the results of the long struggle for Spanish unification was (1) a tradition of religious toleration stemming from the need for Christian unity in the face of Muslim power; (2) a legacy of warlike spirit and national pride; (3) a national heritage of pride in crafts and manual labor that helped stimulate the national economy; (4) Muslim culture was essentially eradicated in Spain; (5) all of the above.

17. _____ A major goal of the Hohenstaufen dynasty was (1) the unification of Spain and Portugal; (2) the expulsion of the Moors from Spain; (3) driving the Mongols from Russia; (4) work with the Lombards to control Italy; (5) none of the above.

18. _____ The term referring to a "guild of learners, both teachers and students" is (1) academy; (2) university; (3) institute; (4) college; (5) union.

19. _____ Thomas Aquinas, author of *Summa Theologica*, sought to (1) reconcile faith and reason; (2) show that Aristotle was wrong; (3) establish a strict doctrine; (4) eliminate heretics from the church; (5) reform the church.

20. _____ Hildegard of Bingen is a good example of (1) an able military leader; (2) an accomplished medieval vocalist (3) an outstanding scholar; (4) a leading critic of the church; (5) a famous architect.

21. _____ The Byzantine brothers, Cyril and Methodius, (1) brought Orthodox Christianity to the Slavic people; (2) translated the liturgy into the Slavic language; (3) devised a Slavic alphabet based on the Greek; (4) led a mission to Moravia (5) all of the above.

22. _____ Nation building in the Balkans lagged behind that in western Europe in large measure because of (1) the ambitions of Russia; (2) the presence of the Ottoman Turks; (3) repeated Mongolian invasions; (4) Bohemian imperialism; (5) the interference of the French.

23. _____ The eastern European peoples within the Orthodox Christian orbit include all of the following EXCEPT (1) Bulgarian; (2) Serbs; (3) Russians; (4) Montenegrins; (5) Croats.

24. _____ The eastern European peoples within the Roman Catholic orbit include all of the following EXCEPT (1) Transylvanians; (2) Poles; (3) Czechs; (4) Croats; (5) Moldavians.

25. _____ The Slavic peoples within the Roman Catholic sphere (1) were knit together by the Latin language; (2) joined in obedience to the papacy; (3) remained culturally linked to western Europe; (4) did not assimilate easily with other groups; (5) all of the above.

26. _____ Regarding the Russian city of Novgorod, choose by number which of the following is correct: (a) it was saved from destruction by the Mongols in the thirteenth century by Alexander Nevsky; (b) it was ruled by an absolute hereditary monarch; (c) it fought off the Teutonic Knights; (d) it declined due to class conflict and diminished Baltic commerce. (1) b; (2) a, c, and d; (3) c and d; (4) a and d; (5) b and d.

RELATIONSHIPS IN TIME

Place each of the items below in correct order under the proper century in the spaces that follow.

Norman Conquest
Charles Martel defeats Muslims at Tours
Magna Carta
Viking raids and settlement across Europe
Venerable Bede writes *Ecclesiastical History of the English People*
Pope Urban II proclaims the First Crusade
Division of the Carolingian Empire
Establishment of the Inquisition
Pontificate of Gregory I
Boethius writes *The Consolation of Philosophy*
Election of Hugh Capet
Charlemagne crowned emperor by the Pope
Clovis unites Franks into one kingdom
Papacy of Gregory VII
Benedictine Rule becomes basic for monastic life

Sixth Century

Seventh Century

Eighth Century

Ninth Century

Tenth Century

Eleventh Century

Twelfth Century

Thirteenth Century

MAKING CONNECTIONS

Explain what happened in each of the following incidents.

Missionaries spread Christianity to England, Ireland, and France

The Donation of Pepin

Charlemagne crowned Emperor of the Romans

The murder of Thomas à Becket

What common theme connects all of these events? What would be the result of these developments for Europe?

FOCUSING ON MAJOR TOPICS

The Feudal System

The collapse of effective central authority, especially following the breakup of Charlemagne's empire, left a political void that was filled by _____.

On the triangle below, indicate how feudal hierarchy theoretically worked. Who was at the top?

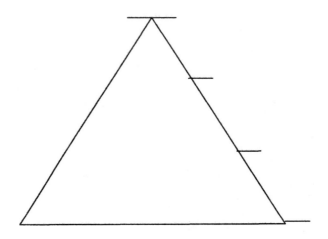

Who was at the bottom of the feudal hierarchy?

Why was the reality of the feudal hierarchy not so simple?

How could one person be both a lord and a vassal?

How could even a king be a vassal?

What did the lords demand from their vassals?

What did the vassals demand from their lords?

What were the three classes of medieval society?

DO YOU KNOW THE SIGNIFICANCE OF THESE TERMS?

The following terms discussed in the chapter are representative of major trends and tendencies in the period. Give the definition for each and, in the space provided, record your opinion of their historical significance.

Boniface

Pepin

Cassiodorus

missi dominici

Carolingian Renaissance

Treaty of Verdun

feudalism

chivalry

oath of fealty

Magna Carta

Cluniac reform

crusader states

Scholasticism

Slavic peoples

Kiev Rus'

MAKING CONNECTIONS

Explain what happened in the Investiture Struggle.

What common theme runs through each of these episodes?

What is the difference between Parliament and *parlement*?

From the point of view of centralizing control of the nation, compare what William the Conqueror did with what the Capetian kings achieved.

THE PLACE

A.   *On the following map, indicate areas in which missionaries Ulfilas, St. Patrick, and Boniface were successful in their efforts to spread Christianity.*

B.   *Indicate with \\\\\\ the extent of Charlemagne's Empire by the time of his death.*

C.   *Mark and label the location of the following: Rome, Paris, Verdun, Aachen, Ravenna, Prague, and Tours.*

D.   *Label each of the following kingdoms: East Franks, West Franks, Byzantine Empire, Khanate of Bulgaria, Umayyad Emirate of Cordova, Ireland, and Danelaw English Kingdom.*

ARRIVING AT CONCLUSIONS

Here are some quotations from eminent scholars dealing with aspects of this period of history. Answer the accompanying questions and be prepared to defend your position.

1. "Was the collapse of the [Carolingian] Empire inherent in the system, in that too much local power was given to the aristocracy without adequate safeguards? Or was it rather the crisis in the structure of leadership at the very top which enabled weaknesses to show themselves?

    "Historians, with their usual prejudice in favour of any type of centralised government, have tended to regard the collapse of the Carolingian Empire as a disaster—an echo of scholarly reaction to the fall of the Roman Empire. The Roman Empire . . . had generally been conceived as a political unit; the Carolingian Empire . . . rarely was. Under the first emperor, Charlemagne, there were three subordinate kings. In 806 Charlemagne ruled for the succession in such a way that, if all his sons had survived, the title of Emperor and the unity of Empire would have disappeared on his death. The survival of the Empire was almost as accidental as its creation." (Edward James, *The Origins of France: From Clovis to the Capetians, 500–1000* [New York: St. Martin's Press, 1982], p. 166.)

How would you reply to the questions the author raises above? What was Charlemagne's conception of imperial authority? How did his idea differ from Constantine's?

2. Orderic Vitalis (1075–1142), the principal historian writing about England under the Normans early in the twelfth century, composed the following dramatic death-bed speech which he attributed to William the Conqueror. "I name no man my heir to the kingdom of England; instead I entrust it to the eternal Creator to whom I belong and in whose hands are all things. For I did not come to possess such dignity by hereditary right, but wrested the kingdom from the perjured Harold with bitter strife and terrible bloodshed, and subjected it to my rule after killing and driving into exile all his supporters. I treated the native inhabitants of the kingdom with unreasonable severity, cruelly oppressed high and low, unjustly disinherited many, and caused the death of thousands by starvation and war, especially in Yorkshire." (Marjorie Chibnall, *The World of Orderic Vitalis* [Oxford: Clarendon Press, 1984], pp. 184–85.)

How does Orderic's assessment of William's reign compare with the one in the text? Orderic was Anglo-Saxon on his mother's side. Has that influenced his judgment? Orderic was also a monk, a member of the clergy. How can that be inferred from the speech?

3. "No one ever spoke of the good times of Philip the Fair as they did of the good times of St. Louis. . . . There were no civil wars in Philip's reign, no notable acts of treason, no executions of famous men, no plunderings of towns and villages. Philip drew heavily on the political capital accumulated by his ancestors, but he also replenished it. He was king of France in a way that none of his predecessors had been. He had forced the most independent lords . . . to recognize his superiority. His courts, and especially . . . the Parlement, retained their reputation for justice." It was Philip's policy of oppressive taxation that "his people could not forgive." (Joseph R. Strayer, *The Reign of Philip the Fair* [Princeton, NJ: Princeton University Press, 1980], p. 423.)

What notable breaches of justice and equity by Philip does the above assessment overlook? Draw your own comparison of Louis IX and Philip the Fair. Why did Philip resort to oppressive fiscal measures?

QUESTIONS TO THINK ABOUT

1. How would you explain the success of Charlemagne? What would be the long-term effects of his interest in intellectual and artistic matters?

2. What is your assessment of the importance of the presence of the Byzantine Empire, Muslim powers, and nomadic tribes surrounding Europe in this period? How did they contribute to the development of feudalism?

3. What were similarities and differences in the daily lives of the clergy, the nobility, and the peasantry in the Early Middle Ages? What does this tell us about the era?

4. How did the objectives and role of the Catholic Church change as the Church expanded into northern and western Europe during the period 500–1000?

5. Why did the Church experience so much difficulty after its period of revival in the eleventh through the thirteenth centuries?

7. What differences did the Norman Conquest make in the subsequent history of England and France? Were the consequences all beneficial for France?

8. What political factors were present in Spain during these centuries that were not present in France and England?

9. Why did a centralized monarchy not develop in Italy and Germany, while it did in England and France?

10. We sometimes hesitate to consider Russia as a European nation. How does knowledge of its early history help us understand Russia's different line of development?

11. The study of history provides us with a more complete understanding of the issues and problems confronting the modern world. Can you identify any contemporary problems or conflicts that are rooted in the ambitions, actions, choices, or philosophical ideals adopted by the peoples who lived during this crucial period of European history? What role did geography play in the events we have studied?

CHAPTER 10

Culture, Power, and Trade in the Era of Asian Hegemony, 220–1350

This chapter describes the beginning of the maturation of civilizations in India and China as well as the ongoing development of civilization in Japan. It shows how the Mongol conquest impacted these civilizations. The Gupta age in India and the Tang and Sung dynasties in China brought full shape to all the elements of civilization. They absorbed ideas from other cultures. Hinduism borrowed from Buddhism while Neo-Confucianism borrowed from Taoism and Buddhism. There was an outpouring of scientific, technological, literary, and artistic creativity, which made these countries the leading lights of the world at a time when the West was still in its "dark ages."

Political disruption and warfare can, of course, be disruptive. The Hinduism that demonstrated such creativity under the Guptas turned inward and defensive when faced with the challenge of Islam. Solidifying the caste system rituals prevented Hindus from converting to Islam in large numbers but also forfeited intellectual creativity. The Mongol conquest swept China off its cultural foundations but also founded a new dynasty that assimilated existing cultural traditions and spread trade and government over an extensive area connecting Asia and Europe.

In other parts of Asia, there were significant developments as well. Never conquered, the Japanese chose the civilization they wanted from Tang China and when, after three centuries, their Chinese-style imperial government began to weaken, they reacted in a similarly purposeful way. Instead of seeking to restore a golden age as the Chinese had, they evolved a new political system based on a feudal dictatorship, the Kamakura Shogunate. Meanwhile, the Korean culture continued to blossom and moved politically from three kingdoms to one. In Oceania, the diverse Pacific island cultures developed their own unique characteristics influenced by the Lapita culture.

YOU SHOULD HAVE A BASIC UNDERSTANDING OF:

The Gupta Empire in India with its remarkable science, literature, and overall influence on other parts of Asia.

The Muslim invasions of India that led to the powerful Delhi Sultanate, which was destroyed by Tamerlane.

The Tang and Sung dynasties with their effective governments, skilled poets, artists, and religious philosophers.

The Mongol Empire, whose military might imposed a *Pax Mongolica* through Asia from China to the Danube River.

Early developments in Korea and its emergence as a kingdom, from three kingdoms into one.

The buildup of a Japanese imperial state out of a competing group of clans, the decline of that form of government, and the emergence of a new structure embodied in the Kamakura Shogunate.

The emergences of three regional Pacific island societies.

HAVE YOU MASTERED THE BASIC FACTS?

Fill in each of the following blanks with the correct identification.

India

1. _____: Dynasty under which Indian culture achieved its classical age.

2. _____: Classical language of Indian written literature.

3. _____: Religion that, after undergoing a revival, became the dominant religion in India during the Gupta period.

4. _____: Separate kingdom in southwest India with extensive overseas contacts.

5. _____: Location of a monumental series of temples carved out of solid rock in India.

6. _____: Muslim conqueror of northwest India known for both his destructiveness and sponsorship of scholars.

7. _____: India's best-known poet and dramatist who wrote the play *Shakuntala*.

8. _____: The most famous Gupta scientist, astronomer-mathematician.

9. _____: Strong Hindu leader who restored unity to North India briefly until his death in 647.

10. _____: Descendants of Central Asian invaders who carved out kingdoms for themselves in the seventh century.

11. _____: Turko-Mongol conqueror who destroyed the Delhi Sultanate in 1398.

12. _____: Indian spoken language synthesizing Persian, Arabic, and Turkish words.

China

13. _____: Term used to refer to the adoption of Chinese civilization and culture, governance, philosophy, and economic organization.

14. _____: Powerful and capable female ruler who expanded the Tang state but was judged harshly in Chinese histories.

15. _____: The name of a Buddhist sect that developed in the fourth century based on the notion of salvation through faith.

16. _____: This Tang ruler both contributed to the prosperity of his government but also to its decline.

17. _____: Eleventh-century Chinese economist and statesman who promoted government policies similar to those of the modern welfare state.

18. _____: Leader of a rebellion in Tang China that fatally weakened the dynasty.

19. _____: School of Chinese thought whose greatest advocate was Chu Hsi; it dominated Chinese intellectual life from the twelfth century to modern times.

20. _____: Chinese dynasty of the seventh to the tenth centuries, which represents the golden age of poetry, painting, scholarship, and political expansion.

21. _____: Method of printing invented in China about 600.

22. _____: Mongol leader who, by 1206, had conquered Mongolia and thereafter pillaged China; overran southern Manchuria; and invaded India, Persia, and Russia.

23. _____: Progressive Mongol leader who ruled China when that land was visited by Westerners in the thirteenth century.

24. _____: Venetian traveler whose account of his journeys to India and China and long stay there provides much of our information on thirteenth-century Asia.

25. _____: Name of the first "barbarian" dynasty to rule all of China.

26. _____: Imperial capital of the Mongols in Central Asia.

27. _____: Chinese city in which one million residents were slaughtered by the Mongols in 1236.

28. _____: During his reign, the Mongols conquered eastern Tibet and Korea.

29. _____: This Franciscan missionary attracted thousands of converts to Christianity between his arrival in Beijing in 1289 and his death in 1322.

Korea, Japan

30. _____: The kingdom in northeast Korea, which first united the country in 668.

31. _____: The name for people who controlled the military and the bureaucracy in Korea.

32. _____: Japanese clan on Honshu Island that was probably the first ruling dynasty of Japan.

33. _____: Traditional Japanese religion based on animistic cults and nature worship.

34. _____: Military-like leaders who ruled Japan after the twelfth century.

35. _____: Japanese warrior nobility who practiced a code of chivalry.

36. _____: Center of Japanese political life from the eighth century to the twelfth century.

37. _____: The most important literary work of the Heian period, perhaps in all of Japanese literature.

38. _____: Japan's first capital city.

39. _____: The racy, amusing, and satirical essays which give good insights to Japanese court life, written by Sei Shonagon, contemporary rival of Lady Murasaki.

40. _____: Dating to the seventh century, Japan's earliest wooden temple compound.

41. _____: Japanese form of Chan Buddhism; popular with the samurai.

42. _____: "Divine winds," they helped save the Japanese from the Mongolian invasion of 1274..

Oceania

43. _____: Pacific island noted for its large stone heads, carved by skilled Polynesian artisans beginning about 1000-1100.

44. _____, _____, and _____: These areas have been considered Oceania since a French explorer coined the term in the 1820s.

TRY THESE MULTIPLE-CHOICE QUESTIONS

1. _____ Chandra Gupta I was (1) a Buddhist monk who helped spread Buddhism into China; (2) a leading Hindu philosopher who reformed Hinduism in the seventh century; (3) an Afghan king who conquered northern India; (4) the founder of the Gupta dynasty; (5) none of the above.

2. _____ Which of the following began FIRST? (1) Song dynasty; (2) Mongol conquest of northern China; (3) Tang dynasty; (4) Jin dynasty; (5) Ming dynasty.

3. _____ In the third century C.E., Chinese chroniclers found the Japanese to be (1) governed by both female and male shamanistic rulers; (2) fond of alcohol; (3) interested in divination; (4) all of the above; (5) none of the above.

4. _____ The Gupta age in India included all of the following characteristics EXCEPT (1) a strengthening of the caste system; (2) a flowering of the arts and literature; (3) a decline in the influence of Hinduism and a corresponding increase in the influence of Buddhism; (4) remarkable advances in science and technology; (5) effects due to the *Bhagavad-Gita*.

5. _____ Which of the following was NOT characteristic of the reform program of Wang Anshih? (1) The government controlled commodity prices and interest rates; (2) Examinations stressed practical rather than literary knowledge; (3) The program was supported by scholars; (4) The reforms were done away with within a generation; (5) Old-age pensions were established.

6. _____ Li Bo and Du Fu have in common that both were (1) early travelers in India who took written reports back to China; (2) among the first writers of objective history in China; (3) Tang poets; (4) Song philosophers; (5) none of the above.

7. _____ Comparing the Gupta monarchy with the Mauryan, the Gupta (1) used none of the political structure of the Mauryan; (2) avoided using secret service spies; (3) depended more on local communal institutions than did the Mauryan; (4) had more extensive royal lands than did the Mauryan; (5) insisted on adopting Buddhism as the official state religion.

8. _____ The Taika reforms in Japan were largely concerned with (1) extending the authority of the priesthood; (2) increasing the power of the clans; (3) emulating Chinese models of government and society; (4) decentralized economic control; (5) all of the above.

9. _____ The *Pax Mongolica* (1) linked Europe and Asia through the Mongol Empire; (2) was a period of armed truce between the Huns and Mongols; (3) marked the extension of Chinese culture into Mesopotamia; (4) saw Muslims in India for the first time; (5) none of the above.

10. _____ Chinese territorial expansion reached its greatest extent during the dynasty of the (1) Sui; (2) Tang; (3) Song; (4) Qin; (5) Xia.

11. _____ China under the Song dynasty included all the following characteristics EXCEPT (1) a revival and reinterpretation of Confucianism; (2) significant advances in experimental and applied sciences; (3) a neglect of painting in favor of architecture; (4) the manufacture of superb pottery; (5) the widespread depiction of the beauty of Nature.

12. _____ King Taejo established this Korean dynasty, which unified the peninsula: (1) Silla; (2) Koguryo; (3) Paekche; (4) Koryŏ; (5) none of the above.

13. _____ Results of the Muslim conquests in India include (1) continuing religious conflict; (2) considerable cultural exchange between Hindu and Muslim; (3) the development of a new religion; (4) all of the above; (5) none of the above.

14. _____ The "Land Below the Wind" refers to: (1) Oceania; (2) today's Malaysia and Indonesia; (3) Japan; (4) Australia; (5) Hong Kong.

15. _____ Which of the following is NOT true about the Kamakura Shogunate? (1) The shogun created his position independently in opposition to the emperor; (2) The shogun was appointed by the emperor; (3) The shogun paid respect to the emperor; (4) The shogun's capital and administration were separate from that of the emperor; (5) The shogun's power rested at least in part on the allegiance of the samurai.

16. _____ Shintō (1) is a complex philosophy with stringent ethics; (2) involves worship of a single deity, the Sun Goddess; (3) clashed violently with Buddhism; (4) supports the divine ancestry of the Japanese imperial line; (5) originated in China.

17. _____ Which of the following was NEVER a part of China at the height of the Tang dynasty? (1) Turkestan; (2) Japan; (3) Yangtse valley; (4) North China Plain; (5) none of the above.

18. _____ Which of the following occurred FIRST? (1) Fujiwara regency; (2) Kamakura Shogunate; (3) building of Kyoto; (4) Taika reforms; (5) the tomb period.

19. _____ The Mongol Empire (1) welcomed foreigners and their ideas; (2) was very suspicious of outsiders; (3) harmed trade among its different parts by its disunity; (4) was easygoing in its governing style; (5) was highly centralized throughout its existence.

DO YOU KNOW THE SIGNIFICANCE OF THESE TERMS?

This chapter contains some terms that may be unfamiliar but are symbolic of larger historical trends and themes. In the space provided, give a definition of each and evaluate each item in terms of its importance for world history.

Faxian

Delhi Sultanate

Sikhism

Tang dynasty

Pure Land Sect

Neo-Confucianism

khanates

Yuan dynasty

Gog and Magog

Three Kingdoms period

pagoda

Yamato clan

Heian period

samurai

Tale of Genji

THE PLACE

A.   *Locate the following on the map that appears on the next page.*

China	Yellow Sea	Kyushu	Pacific Ocean
Japan	Shikoku	Sea of Japan	Honshu
Korea	Hokkaido	Manchuria	Oceania

B.   *Write in these rivers.*

Huang Ho   Yalu   Yangtse

C.   *Place a dot on the map and write the name of each of these cities in the appropriate place.*

Seoul	Tokyo	Kyoto
Peking	Chang'an	

D.   *With this symbol ////// indicate the route of the first Grand Canal. With this symbol ---- show the site of the Great Wall.*

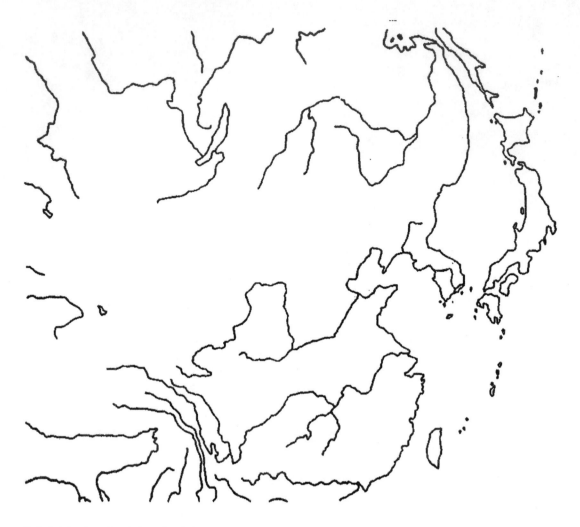

ARRIVING AT CONCLUSIONS

Here are some quotations from eminent scholars dealing with significant matters from this period of history. Answer the accompanying questions briefly and be prepared to defend your position.

1. "Gupta art, the 'classical' art of India, was of tremendous importance for all Buddhist art of Southeast Asia, Central Asia, China, and Japan. It gave that art its norm, and the sculpture and painting of the Gupta period occupy a position parallel to that of Greek and Roman art in the West, in which European artistic canons found their standards of perfection. The final solution of the problems of form and content provided a firm basis for original artistic expression, and whether in Cambodia, Java, or Japan, the powerful yet subtle influence of Gupta art may always be detected." (Woodbridge Bingham, Hilary Conroy, and Frank W. Ikle, *A History of Asia*, vol. I [Boston: Allyn and Bacon, 1964], p. 196.)

What other aspects of Indian culture do you think might have been exported along with the standards of Gupta art? If the analogy between Gupta art in Asia with Greek and Roman art in Europe is valid, what would you expect some of the consequences to be, both in India and elsewhere in Asia where Gupta art standards penetrated?

2. "Endowed with an adequate physical base for the development of its own institutions and traditions, Japan was also profoundly affected by its location on the world map. At its closest point, the island of Kyushu is about 120 miles from the continent, across the Korean Strait. It was over this route that continental influences entered Japan, for direct

contact with China did not become general until late in the seventh century and, even then, remained hazardous. Although conquerors from the mainland may have played an important part in Japan's early history, Japan was too far away to be dominated by mainland powers. Foreign ideas, institutions, and techniques could be adapted to Japanese needs without military or political interference from abroad." (Conrad Schirokauer, *A Brief History of Chinese and Japanese Civilizations* [New York: Harcourt Brace Jovanovich, 1978], p. 131.)

How did the Japanese modify the Chinese institutions that they borrowed? Although they had enough geographic isolation to be able to choose, why do you think they chose to "adapt" rather than just become wholly like the Chinese? *Could they have become just like the Chinese?*

3.   Mongol armies of the thirteenth century conquered vast territories with limited manpower. A famed military historian helps explain their success.

"The best example of strategy in the Middle Ages comes not from the West but from the East. For the thirteenth century, strategically distinguished in the West, was made outstanding by the paralysing lesson in strategy taught by the Mongols to European chivalry. In scale and in quality, in surprise and mobility, in the strategic and tactical indirect approach, their campaigns rival or surpass any in history. In Jenghiz [Genghis] Khan's conquest of China we can trace his use of Taitong Fu to bait successive traps as Bonaparte after utilized the fortress of Mantua. By far-flung movements with a combination of three armies he finally broke up the military and moral cohesion of the Chin empire. When in 1220 he invaded the Karismian empire, whose center of power lay in modern Turkestan, one force distracted the enemy's attention to the approach from Kashgar in the south; then the main mass appeared in the north; screened by its operations, he himself with his reserve army swung wider still and, after disappearing into the Kizyl-Kum desert, debouched by surprise at Bokhara in the rear of the enemy's defensive lines and armies." (B. H. Liddell Hart, *Strategy* [New York: Praeger, 1954], pp. 81–82.)

To what does Liddell Hart attribute the military success of the Mongols? Why would he regard the Mongols as masters of the "indirect approach" in military affairs? How does the quotation suggest that the Mongols sometimes employed techniques similar to those of the Arabs in the seventh and eighth centuries?

QUESTIONS TO THINK ABOUT

1.   If you were preparing an outline for a debate on the merits of the caste system, what leading arguments would you assign to the affirmative? To the negative?

2.   Why do you think India was so swayed and affected by outside invaders, whereas China seemed to absorb Central Asian conquerors and go back to their old ways of doing things? Could it have been because the Chinese did not have to deal with frequent invasion? Or could it have been because the Chinese never had to deal directly with fiercely exclusive thought systems, like Islam, among their invaders?

3.   Why did Buddhism decline in the country of its birth, India, at the same time that it was spreading and prospering in China, Korea, and Japan?

4.   What were the most important historical influences in the shaping of Korea, and how were they manifested?

5.   Japan's obligation to China in terms of its arts, politics, religion, and philosophy has been described as "immense." Do you agree? What are some good and what are some unfortunate results of such cultural diffusion?

6.   What were the long-term effects of Mongol rule? Assess them in terms of productive and destructive effects, and express your opinion.

CHAPTER 11

The Americas to 1500

Contemporary Americans value their rich cultural diversity. Since the late fifteenth century, the cultural diversity of the Western Hemisphere has been shaped by an influx of peoples from Europe, Asia, and Africa. In the process of this migration, the peoples already living in the so-called New World often were conquered, displaced, and decimated. But cultural diversity in the Americas did not begin with the Columbian age. Indeed, the societies that evolved in the Americas in the centuries prior to 1500 were marked by a high degree of cultural variation.

The great Amerindian empires—the Olmecs, Mayas, and Aztecs of Mesoamerica, and the Incas in South America—established strong governing institutions to rule over their large populations. The cultural evolution toward a more centralized political system was made possible by increased agricultural production, which in turn encouraged population growth, the development of large urban centers, the expansion of regional trade, and the elaboration of governing and social institutions. Despite being isolated from the developments taking place in other parts of the world, the evolution of American civilizations followed a similar pattern as that of other civilizations in Eurasia and Africa.

In North America, a different pattern of cultural development took place. Scattered across a broad continent, Amerindian tribes in the north formed smaller, self-sustaining civilizations. The transition from food-gathering to food-producing economies among some of the northern peoples did not result in the formation of large empires, as had occurred in Central and South America. There was great variety among the Amerindian societies in the north, from the Mesolithic cultures of the Inuit and Aleuts in the far Northwest to the more sophisticated Iroquois confederation in the Northeast. Whatever their level of cultural development, all of the Amerindian societies in the Western Hemisphere were affected by European penetration after 1500.

YOU SHOULD HAVE A BASIC UNDERSTANDING OF:

The origins of Amerindian societies.

The major political and social characteristics of the Olmecs, Mayas, Aztecs, and Incas.

The Amerindians of North America.

HAVE YOU MASTERED THE BASIC FACTS?

Fill in each of the following blanks with the correct identification.

Origins of Americans; Civilizations in Mesoamerica and North America

1. _____: Land bridge connecting Alaska and Asia used by Paleolithic hunters to migrate to the Western Hemisphere.

2. _____: The first city in the Americas, founded around 2600 B.C.E. The Pyramids built there may have been constructed a century before the Great Pyramid at Giza in Egypt.

3. _____ : Principal food crop of the native civilizations of the Western Hemisphere.

4. _____ : Early Mesoamerican civilization famous for its large building projects and colossal sculptured stone heads.

5. _____ : Early Central American Indians with a remarkably advanced culture, notable especially for their city-state organization, scientific achievements, and art.

6. _____ : Warlike Indian confederacy controlling Mexico in 1500.

7. _____ : Most advanced of the South American peoples, whose civilization once dominated the western coast of the continent.

8. _____ : Term applied to Mexican and Central American cultures after about 1200 B.C.E.

9. _____ : Capital of the Aztec Empire, an architectural wonder, constructed on an island.

10. _____ and _____ : According to the text, two of the most significant achievements of the Mayans.

11. _____ : Strong-willed ruler of the Aztecs in the fifteenth century, who extended the empire to the Gulf Coast.

12. _____ : Greatest ruler of the Inca Empire, who added worship of a supreme creator to the current cult of the sun.

13. _____ : Major trading center and burial site near present-day East St. Louis, Illinois; it served as a capital for the Amerindian culture in the Mississippi valley.

14. _____ : Religious sites used for worship and human sacrifice.

15. _____ : Toltec capital, founded by King Topiltzin in the tenth century.

16. _____ : System of notation developed by the Mayans for maintaining records.

17. _____ : Appointed nobility in the Aztec Empire.

The Amerindians of North America

18. _____ : North American people who established the League of the Five Nations.

19. _____ and _____ : In the area of present-day Kentucky and Ohio, these cultures were known for burying their dead in earthen mounds and including various precious relics in the mounds.

20. _____ : People who developed a sophisticated culture in the southwest of the present-day United States; they are noted for their architecture, use of irrigation, and weaving of cotton cloth.

21. _____ and _____ : Peoples of the far north; they are more closely related to Asians than other Amerindian peoples.

TRY THESE MULTIPLE-CHOICE QUESTIONS

1. _____ At the time Spanish explorers came to the Western Hemisphere, there were mature civilizations in all of the following areas EXCEPT (1) Mexico; (2) Peru; (3) Tierra del Fuego; (4) Guatemala; (5) none of the above.

2. _____ Amerindian civilizations lacked all of the following EXCEPT (1) iron; (2) horses; (3) pottery; (4) many domesticated animals; (5) the wheel.

3. _____ The Mesoamerican culture that provided the foundation for other cultures that came after it was that of the (1) Aztecs; (2) Olmecs; (3) Toltecs; (4) Incas; (5) Mayans.

4. _____ Which of the following occurred FIRST? (1) the beginning of the Inca Empire; (2) the beginning of the Aztec Empire; (3) construction of the first Mayan cities; (4) foundation of the Olmec civilization; (5) the emergence of a distinct culture among the Iroquois.

5. _____ Of all the New World cultures, the one that came closest to developing an alphabetic system of writing was the (1) Toltec; (2) Maya; (3) Inca; (4) Aztec; (5) Olmec.

6. _____ The Olmec civilization was centered FIRST at (1) La Venta; (2) Teotihuacán; (3) Tenochtitlán; (4) San Lorenzo; (5) Cozumel.

7. _____ Choose by *number* the correct generalizations about Olmec civilization. (a) It originated on the coastal plain of modern Peru. (b) It produced colossal stone heads and carried out large building projects. (c) It was dominated by a priestly class. (d) It was unusually violent and aggressive toward surrounding peoples. (1) a and b; (2) b and c; (3) b, c, and d; (4) only a; (5) c and d.

8. _____ The distinctive characteristics of Inca civilization included all of the following EXCEPT (1) an excellent military system, including compulsory military service; (2) a well-developed monetary and credit system; (3) ceremonial public veneration of mummified emperors; (4) an accurate solar calendar; (5) the belief in a universal Creator.

9. _____ With respect to their political practices and culture, the Aztecs and Mayas have been compared to the (1) Romans and Greeks; (2) Egyptians and Persians; (3) Chinese and Indians; (4) Germans and French; (5) Japanese and Germans.

10. _____ Which of the following was NOT a member of the League of the Five Nations? (1) the Seneca; (2) the Mohawk; (3) the Pueblo; (4) the Oneida; (5) the Onondaga.

11. _____ The postclassical era in Mesoamerica was marked by (1) the decline of artistic expression; (2) the decline of urban populations; (3) increased militarism and war; (4) human sacrifice to the gods; (5) all of the above.

12. _____ Toltec civilization was marked by (1) extensive trade; (2) conquest of neighboring peoples; (3) decreased agricultural production; (4) human sacrifice to the gods; (5) all of the above.

13. _____ Commoners in the Aztec Empire (1) developed a prosperous market system under strict state control; (2) primarily served as slave laborers in the cities; (3) were barred from the ranks of the appointed nobility; (4) could be made nobles by distinguished achievement; (5) none of the above.

107

14. _____Choose by *number* the correct generalizations about Aztec religion. (a) It focused on the worship of the sun-god, Huitzilopochtli. (b) Its focus on human virtue provided the Aztecs with a source of inspiration. (c) Unlike some other Mesoamerican religions, human sacrifice was rare. (d) human sacrifices were necessary to provide the gods with energy. (1) a and b; (2) a and d; (3) a, b, and d; (4) only a; (5) b and c.

15. _____ The Incas were particularly skilled in making all of the following EXCEPT (1) iron weapons; (2) roads; (3) aqueducts; (4) bridges; (5) canals for irrigation.

16. _____ Amerindian societies in North America (1) were more technologically advanced than Mesoamerican societies; (2) varied greatly from one another in language and culture; (3) relied exclusively on hunting and gathering; (4) organized into large empires; (5) none of the above.

17. _____Which of the following peoples lived in what is today the northeastern United States? (1) the Navajo; (2) the Apache; (3) the Cayuga; (4) the Hohokam; (5) the Mandan.

18. _____Which of the following took place FIRST? (1) reign of Pachacuti; (2) Cahokia complex is built; (3) Adena and Hopewell cultures emerge; (4) reign of Montezuma II; (5) the classical period ends.

FOCUSING ON MAJOR TOPICS

Name the three important cultures that flourished in the Americas before the European explorers arrived in great numbers.

Which two cultures were roughly contemporaneous?

Generally speaking, during what centuries did the third culture flourish?

Where was this earlier civilization located?

Which two arts reached a particularly high level of achievement?

Briefly describe the Mayan religion and its importance in the lifestyle of the Mayas.

DO YOU KNOW THE SIGNIFICANCE OF THESE TERMS?
This chapter contains some terms that represent important trends and tendencies in world history. In the space provided, identify and assess the historical significance of each.

Olmec

Pyramid of the Sun

Mayan calendar

ball court

Huitizopochtli

Toltecs

Aztecs

Aztec Sun Stone

Chinampas

Pachacuti

matrilineal

Quechua

Mississippians

Mound Builders

Pueblo

THE PLACE

A.   *On the map on the following page, indicate with a heavy solid line the boundaries of the Mayan Empire and the regions controlled respectively by the Toltecs, Olmec, Iroquois, and Pueblos.*

B.   *Indicate with \\\\\\ the boundaries of the Aztec Empire.*

C.   *Indicate with ////// the boundaries of the Inca Empire.*

D.   *Using the maps in the textbook, locate and mark the following items on the map.*

San Lorenzo	Chimu	Andes Mountains
Monte Alban	Tiahuanaco	Caribbean Sea
Oaxaca	Tenochtitlán	Rio Grande
Cuzco	Huari	Teotihuacán
Mayapan	Machu Picchu	Cahokia

0   250   500 Miles

0   250   500 Kilometers

20° N

0°

20° S

40° S

120° W   100° W   80° W   60° W   40° W   20° W

110

ARRIVING AT CONCLUSIONS

Here are some quotations from scholars dealing with the significance of this period of history. Answer the accompanying questions briefly, and be prepared to defend your position.

1.   "Manipulations of traditional religious concepts and rituals played crucial roles in the rise and fall of the Aztec and Inca Empires. In the second quarter of the fifteenth century Mexican and Inca leaders instituted specific ideological reforms. While these changes were intended to serve certain limited purposes, they also proved to be highly effective adaptations to the natural and cultural environments of Mesoamerica and the Central Andes. . . . The new state religions gave the Mexican and Inca decisive advantages over their competitors and enabled both peoples to conquer vast territories in a remarkably short time. However, in the long run the very same ideological factors created internal cultural stresses . . . that could not be resolved. In less than a century the problems had reached the point of crisis, and what the Spaniards toppled were two states destroying themselves from within." (Geoffrey W. Conrad and Arthur A. Demarest, *Religion and Empire: The Dynamics of Aztec and Inca Expansionism* [New York: Cambridge University Press, 1984], p. 4.)

Would you agree with the authors' contention that religion was chief among many causes for the rise and decline of the two great Amerindian civilizations? Is the evolution of the Aztec and Inca Empires similar to that of the Roman Empire? Is the argument developed above consistent with that presented in the text?

2.   "The history of the Americas records the colonization and settlement of a great continent. We take a just pride in our European ancestors, who, from the Vikings down to the most recent political exiles, set forth to find a new life in the changing conditions of a new land. Our histories and traditions describe the evolution of these colonies into the present group of American republics, and it is a remarkable episode in the story of mankind. Yet the European settlement of the Americas, for all of its modern political significance, is just a late phase of the history of man on the American continent. The Asiatic colonization of the New World, which preceded the European infiltration by many centuries, has its own proud place in the Annals of Continental America." (George C. Vaillant, *The Aztecs of Mexico* [Baltimore: Penguin Books, 1956], p. 23.)

What does Vaillant mean by the "Asiatic colonization of the New World"? Why should a modern American take pride in the accomplishments of the pre-Columbian cultures of America? What aspects of pre-Columbian culture survive today in the American nations?

QUESTIONS TO THINK ABOUT

1.   What similarities and what differences do you find between the Mesoamerican civilizations of before 1500 and the civilizations in sub-Saharan Africa?

2.   Which of the Amerindian civilizations do you consider most interesting? Why?

3.   What was the source of power and authority for the rulers of the Amerindian empires we studied? In what ways were the New World rulers more powerful than their contemporary counterparts in Europe and Asia?

4.   Scholars have been amazed at the incredible accomplishments of the First Americans. What would have happened if they had been left alone for another 500 years?

CHAPTER 12

The Great Dynastic Empires of Eurasia, 1300–1650

One of the recurring themes in history is the cyclical nature of nations and empires. Civilizations are born, reach their zenith under extraordinary leaders, and over time lose their vitality and strength. The remarkable feature in this cycle is that new civilizations emerge out of the decadence of the old, regenerated by new leaders and by outside cultural influences, often resulting in cultural synthesis. Such were the circumstances under which the Ottoman, Safavid, and Mughal empires emerged between 1300 and 1650. Coming on the heels of the Mongol and Timurid conquests in Southwest Asia and Anatolia, new Muslim Turkic dynasties began the process of consolidating and extending their realms with military might enhanced by the use of gunpowder weaponry.

Conquering an empire is not synonymous with establishing imperial authority, and the rulers of the new empires faced a monumental task in establishing an effective governing structure for their domains. Built upon the foundations of pre-existing cultural institutions and ethnically diverse populations, the most outstanding emperors realized that the vitality of their empires required a considerable degree of toleration for their non-Muslim subjects—an ideal that stood in sharp contrast to the policies adopted by their contemporary counterparts in Christian Europe.

In the sixteenth century, the Asian empires were clearly ascendant, controlling the East–West trade routes and drawing on the ample resources and manpower existing within their realms. Emperors also encouraged artistic endeavors, which endure both as expressions of cultural synthesis and as evidence of imperial greatness. But in the latter half of the seventeenth century, the Islamic "gunpowder empires" began to decline. Significant factors include the degeneration in the character of ruling dynasties, the increasing inefficiency and ineffectiveness of governing institutions over time, and deviation from policies that drew on the strengths of multiculturalism and ethnic diversity as pillars of the imperial system.

YOU SHOULD HAVE A BASIC UNDERSTANDING OF:

The regional political, economic, and cultural circumstances that contributed to the rise of the Ottoman, Safavid, and Mughul empires.

The important rulers of each empire and their achievements.

The role religion played in advancing the authority of rulers.

The rivalry between the Muslim empires and their relationships with outside powers.

The distinctive social, cultural, and political characteristics of each empire, as well as their shared characteristics.

HAVE YOU MASTERED THE BASIC FACTS?

Fill in each of the following blanks with the correct identification.

Ottoman Empire

1. _____: Region in the Near East, bordered by the eastern Mediterranean, Aegean, and Black Seas; it was the heart of the Ottoman Empire.

2. _____: Formerly the capital of the Byzantine Empire, the Ottomans conquered the city in 1453, made it their imperial capital, and renamed it Istanbul.

3. _____: Ottoman sultan who led the troops who conquered the city identified above; he also took control over Romania and the regions surrounding the Crimea.

4. _____: The founder of the Ottoman ruling dynasty.

5. _____: Fourteenth-century emir of the Chaghatai Khanate in central Asia, his ambition to restore the grandeur of the Mongol Empire led to a series of campaigns in the Crimea, Persia, and Anatolia.

6. _____: Probably the greatest Ottoman sultan, he added new territory to his empire at the expense of the European Habsburgs and Persian Safavids, and he established new laws and administrative structures to govern his extensive multicultural empire.

7. _____: Institution of slavery based on a "human tax" of boys from non-Muslim subjects; they were trained to serve as elite infantry troops, and many rose to high positions in the Ottoman imperial system.

8. _____: The Ottoman sultan's chief minister, he served as the head of the government's central bureaucracy.

9. _____: Great palace built during the reign of Sultan Mehmed II; its architectural design mirrored the Byzantine style.

10. _____: Term for non-Muslim subjects in the Ottoman Empire who were allowed a considerable degree of religious and civil autonomy under responsible local religious leaders.

Safavid Empire

11. _____: Founder of the Safavid ruling dynasty.

12. _____: Early sixteenth-century Safavid shah, renowned for both his military and governing skills; he united Persia, conquered Iraq, and challenged the Ottomans in eastern Anatolia.

13. _____: Mystical Shi'ite order from which Shah Ismail was alleged to have gained secret religious insight, giving him the aura of quasi-divine power.

14. _____: This shah's reign was the "golden age" of the Safavid Empire; he encouraged the arts, created a stable political system, and gained security through wise statesmanship.

15. _____: Poet of the masterpiece *Epic of Kings* (*Shahnamah*).

Mughul Empire

16. _____: Ruler of Kabul who established the foundations of the Mughul Empire in a series of conquests against regional rivals in the early sixteenth century.

s17. _____: Famous tomb built during the seventeenth century at Agra for the wife of Shah Jahan.

18. _____: Perhaps the greatest Mughul emperor, he added territory to his empire through conquest, established an effective governing administration, promoted cultural and religious toleration, and encouraged the arts.

19. _____: Military administrators who served both in governing positions and in the Mughul emperor's army.

20. _____: Mughul emperor who defeated his brother in a struggle to succeed Shah Jahan; after gaining the throne, he imposed Sunni Muslim orthodoxy over his dominions.

21. _____: Major trading center located between India and Persia, it served as a central point in the East–West trade.

22. _____: Uzbek ruler defeated by Shah Ismail in 1510; Ismail subsequently fashioned a drinking cup out of his skull.

TRY THESE MULTIPLE-CHOICE QUESTIONS

1. _____ The imperial power nominally ruling most of Anatolia during the time of Osman was (1) Kurdistan; (2) the Seljuk Turks; (3) the Byzantine Empire; (4) the Holy Roman Empire; (5) the Umayyads.

2. _____ In the late fourteenth century, Timur's military campaigns reached into all of the following regions EXCEPT (1) Anatolia; (2) Persia; (3) India; (4) Egypt; (5) Austria.

3. _____ As a means of legitimizing their rule, Ottoman Sultans claimed to be descendants of (1) Genghis Khan; (2) Constantine the Great; (3) the Prophet Muhammad; (4) Timur; (5) Ali.

4. _____ During the sixteenth century, Suleiman's rule was characterized by (1) dramatic expansionism; (2) harsh response to challenges to his authority; (3) a lavish lifestyle; (4) demands that foreign dignitaries recognize his dominance; (5) all of the above.

5. _____ Hungary was absorbed by the Ottoman Empire in 1526 following the bloody battle at (1) Mohacs; (2) island of Rhodes; (3) Prague; (4) Kosovo; (5) Belgrade.

6. _____ The institution of slavery as practiced in the Ottoman Empire (1) produced a permanent class of servile labor for whom there was little chance of upward mobility; (2) was a means by which the empire gained talented individuals to serve in the military and in administrative positions for the government; (3) relied to the greatest extent on Muslim prisoners of war; (4) was based on race; (5) all of the above.

7. _____ After 1600, Ottoman power faced several setbacks, including (1) a series of costly wars with Persia that ended in stalemate; (2) renewed military threats from Russia and the Habsburgs in Europe; (3) a decline of naval strength in the Red Sea; (4) cheap silver from the Americas having a negative economic effect; (5) all of the above.

115

8. _____ The Ottoman victory against Ismail's Safavid forces in 1514 (1) tainted Ismail's reputation of invincibility; (2) was a result of the Ottoman forces' advantage in gunpowder weaponry; (3) was followed by additional conflicts between the two powers; (4) demoralized Ismail; (5) all of the above.

9. _____ Which of the following Safavid shahs immediately succeeded Ismail? (1) Tahmasp; (2) Abbas; (3) Safi al-Din; (4) Nader; (5) Bayezid II.

10. _____ Which of the following was NOT a significant Persian export in the East–West trade? (1) silk; (2) salt; (3) ceramics; (4) carpets; (5) porcelain.

11. _____ Prior to Ismail's reign in the early sixteenth century, the religion most Persians embraced was (1) Shi'ite Islam; (2) Sunni Islam; (3) Greek Orthodox Christianity; (4) Hinduism; (5) Sufism.

12. _____ Choose the number at the end of this question that most accurately describes the attitude of the Safavid rulers toward artistic and cultural achievement. (a) Although Ismail supported the arts, his successors contributed little support to cultural projects. (b) During the reign of Shah Abbas, Persia became one of the primary cultural centers of the world. (c) Persian excellence in architecture is reflected in the awe-inspiring majesty of the Shah's palace at Isfahan. (d) Due to strict interpretation of Muslim law, the Safavids never developed original art forms. (1) only b; (2) a, b, and c; (3) b and c; (4) only a; (5) a, b, c, and d.

13. _____ Akbar's reign was successful in promoting which of the following? (1) a synthesis of Hindu and Muslim cultures; (2) a flowering of artistic achievement and learning; (3) growing prosperity in trade and increased industrial production; (4) the view of himself as a pragmatic monarch; (5) all of the above.

14. _____ All of the following characteristics are common in Mughul architecture EXCEPT (1) flying buttresses; (2) vaulted gateways; (3) domes; (4) mosaics; (5) fusion of Iranian and Indic styles.

15. _____ The *Din-i-Ilahi* was (1) a tax imposed on non-Muslim subjects; (2) a great Sanskrit epic; (3) a religious cult proclaimed by Akbar; (4) a palace built during the reign of Babur; (5) a monumental temple.

16. _____ Choose the number at the end of this question that explains the cause of the Mughul Empire's decline during the seventeenth century. (a) Akbar's successors became embroiled in unsuccessful military campaigns that sapped the empire's economic strength. (b) After Akbar's death, Muslim Sufi orders and the *ulama* pressured his successors to govern according to Islamic law. (c) Aurangzeb's reimposition of the Sharia and the *jizya* alienated the predominantly Hindu population of the empire. (d) European commercial domination over the Indian Sea trade routes quickly expanded over the Persian Gulf region. (1) b; (2) a and c; (3) c and d; (4) a, b, and c; (5) a, b, c, and d.

17. _____ The most significant source of income for the Ottoman, Safavid, and Mughul empires was (1) agricultural production; (2) control over the East–West trade routes; (3) export of gold and ceramics; (d) export of textiles; (5) none of the above.

18. _____ Compared to the most advanced European states of the sixteenth century, the Ottoman, Safavid, and Mughul empires enjoyed an advantage in all of the following areas EXCEPT (1) imperial wealth; (2) technological development; (3) manpower and resources; (4) effective governing systems; (5) none of the above.

FOCUSING ON MAJOR TOPICS

In the blank before each of the following items, write an O to indicate a characteristic of the Ottoman Empire, an S to indicate a characteristic of the Safavid Empire, or an M to indicate a characteristic of the Mughul Empire. Some characteristics may apply to more than one empire, so mark them accordingly.

1. _____ Troops wore red headgear with 12 folds as a symbol of their Shi'ite faith.

2. _____ A majority of its citizens were Hindu.

3. _____ Ruled by a Turkic dynasty.

4. _____ Silk, ceramics, and carpets were its major exports.

5. _____ Fratricide (the execution of one's brothers) was a common aspect of dynastic succession.

6. _____ Capital was at Isfahan.

7. _____ Society was patriarchal.

8. _____ Foreign-born Muslims called *mansabdars* served as military administrators for the empire.

9. _____ Elite infantry corps was called the janissaries.

10. _____ Primary European rival was the Habsburgs Empire.

11. _____ Competed with Portugal for control of the East–West trade.

12. _____ Employed a "human tax" on non-Muslim subjects to staff the military and government bureaucracy.

13. _____ Sufi mysticism exerted considerable influence within the empire.

14. _____ Originally predominantly Sunni but became overwhelmingly Shi'ite under its ruling dynasty.

Here are three significant rulers we have studied. Give a brief sketch of each, identifying his major accomplishments.

Shah Abbas "the Great"   Suleiman "the Great"   Akbar

DO YOU KNOW THE SIGNIFICANCE OF THESE TERMS?

This chapter contains some terms that may be unfamiliar. Write a short definition of each and state the historical significance for world history.

Osman

Suleiman

tughra

janissaries

harem

Topkapi Palace

Safavid dynasty

Shah Abbas

Isfahan

Mughul Empire

Akbar

Taj Mahal

Hamzanamah

sati

Kabul

THE PLACE

A.   *On the following outline map, indicate by a heavy line the boundaries of the Ottoman Empire at the end of the sixteenth century.*

B.   *Indicate with \|\|\|\|\|\|\| the area ruled by the Safavid Empire at the end of the sixteenth century.*

C.   *Indicate with ////// the region ruled by the Mughul Empire by the end of the seventeenth century.*

D.   *Locate and mark each of the following items on the map.*

Anatolia	Arabian Sea
Red Sea	Egypt
Isfahan	Fatehpur Sikri
Persian Gulf	Vijayanagar
Iraq	Black Sea
Delhi	Cairo
Deccan	Mediterranean Sea
Persia	Mecca
Kabul	Caspian Sea
Istanbul	Tabriz

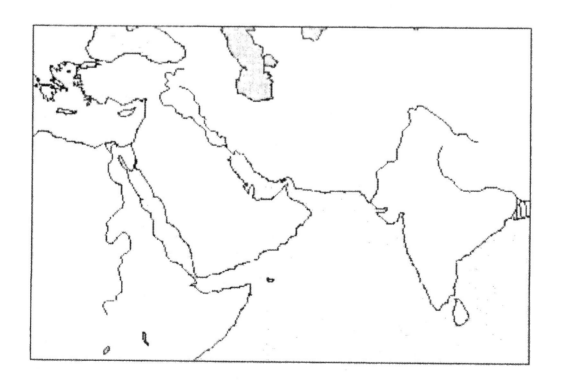

119

ARRIVING AT CONCLUSIONS

Here are some quotes from scholars dealing with the significance of this period of history. Answer the accompanying questions briefly, and be prepared to defend your position.

1.   "Suleiman's reforms, for all their liberal intentions and principles, were inevitably limited in their effect by the fact that he was legislating from above, with the advice only of a small circle of high officials and jurists. Remote in their capital from the bulk of his widely scattered subjects, . . . he was not in a position either to consult them directly as to the likely effects of his legislation upon them, or to follow it through and ensure its just enforcement, abuses, to a degree of official corruption fraught with hazards for the future." (Lord Kinross, *The Ottoman Centuries* [New York: Morrow Quill, 1977], pp. 210–11.)

What fundamental problems within the Ottoman governing system does Kinross identify? To what extent were these problems inevitable given the state of technology during the sixteenth century and the large, multicultural empire ruled by the Ottomans? In what ways could the Ottomans' governing system have been improved even under these conditions? Explain.

2.   "[Akbar] astutely recognized political reality in an empire in which 80 to 90 per cent of the population was non-Muslim—predominantly Hindu, but also Jain, animist, Christian, Jewish, and Zoroastrian. The Mughals were a Turco-Mongol garrison state that controlled the urban centres and agricultural heartlands of the Indo-Gangetic fertile crescent. Mughal emperors exercised a fragile paramountcy over a bewildering variety of Hindu and Muslim rulers who, like the Rajputs, Afghans, and Marathas of west-central India, had deep roots in the countryside. The Mughal's Timurid identity did not legitimize their rule in the eyes of most South Asian inhabitants, and even their Islamic faith was not sufficient to co-opt Afghan clans for more than temporary service." (Stephen F. Dale, "The Islamic World in the Age of European Expansion, 1500–1800," in *The Cambridge Illustrated History of the Islamic World*, ed. Francis Robinson [Cambridge: Cambridge University Press, 1996], pp. 79–80.)

What policies did Akbar adopt to rule his multicultural empire? What did Dale mean when he described the Mughul Empire as a "garrison state"? What cultural factors, other than those stemming from religion and faith, presented problems for the Mughul rulers? What lessons can modern multicultural societies learn from the Mughul Empire's example?

QUESTIONS TO THINK ABOUT

1. Explain why the empires studied in this chapter are called "gunpowder empires." Is this an accurate description? Why or why not?

2. Are there similarities between the policies adopted by Ottoman sultan Suleiman I and Mughul emperor Akbar? In what ways did each ruler approach the problems of ruling a diverse, multiethnic empire differently?

3. Trade and commerce was a primary concern for the Ottoman, Safavid, and Mughul rulers. To what extent were the emperors of these states able to control the trade routes through their territory? What factors contributed to European dominance over the region's commerce and trade by the seventeenth century?

4. Although the Ottoman sultanate ruled well into the twentieth century, can you identify any fundamental weaknesses in its governing system apparent as early as the seventeenth century that might have contributed to its decline? Explain.

5. Why did effective government in the Ottoman, Safavid, and Mughul empires rely to such a great extent on the character and humanity of their rulers?

CHAPTER 13

East Asian Cultural and Political Systems, 1300–1650

In this chapter, we see important changes in areas of Asia that shared mutual influences, with regard to their governments, economies, and cultures. The rise, growth, and decline of the Ming dynasty in China and those of Korea, Japan, and Southeast Asia are all covered by the text's discussion dealing with the time period from the fourteenth to the middle of the seventeenth centuries.

China, in the sense of Chinese civilization, often called the Central Flower, was still the dominant influence throughout the period as trade, social, and cultural interaction still very much connected east Asia together. At the same time, China, the Central Kingdom, the political entity, exercised a broad influence on surrounding developing nation-states, largely in the form of the tribute system and generally in its efforts to act as a kind of protective parent. It continued to cast a giant shadow across east Asia at the time new nations there continued to define themselves.

Korea continued its development as a nation under the Choson dynasty, still showing Chinese influences, paying tribute to China but retaining its indigenous identity, and further assimilating neo-Confucianism. In Japan, internal changes in the leadership of shogunate rule were accompanied by cultural achievements at the same time Japan began to feel some pressure from European contact. By 1600, a new shogunate, the Tokugawa Shogunate, arose, controlling Japan to the middle of the nineteenth century. In Southeast Asia, contending states, affected historically by contact with India and China, maintained a strong sense of identity and continued in their efforts to work out their independence even as they competed with neighboring states. There, too, European intrusion began to be an ever increasing factor as outside forces worked to make their presence known economically and culturally throughout the region.

YOU SHOULD HAVE A BASIC UNDERSTANDING OF:

The characteristics of Chinese culture under the Ming dynasty.

Korea: the making of a Confucian society.

What Japan was like during the Ashikaga and early Tokugawa shogunates.

The geographical influences on Southeast Asia, the outside influences that determined its direction, and the pattern of rivalries that kept the region divided.

HAVE YOU MASTERED THE BASIC FACTS?

Fill in each of the following blanks with the correct identification.

China

1. _____: A branch of the White Lotus Society that used Buddhist, Confucian, and Daoist ideas, it was a religious-based political group.

2. _____: The title under which the rebel monk Zhu Yuanzhang ruled as emperor.

3. _____: Castrated males who served as palace attendants and administrators for the Chinese emperors.

4. _____: This emperor pressed China's influence outside its borders and sponsored a series of naval expeditions.

5. _____: This practice, thought to enhance female beauty, became increasingly widespread in Ming China.

6. _____: This practice brought young females into richer households.

7. _____: Chinese semisatirical novel in which a monk travels with animals.

8. _____: Chinese novel that was the counterpart of Robin Hood's activities.

9. _____: Ming China's best-known ceramic achievement was in this medium.

10. _____: Produced by over 2,000 scholars who arranged more than 7,000 works by subjects into more than 22,000 chapters.

11. _____: The Portugese trading base in China was at this port.

12. _____: Erudite Roman Catholic missionary order active in Ming China and Japan.

13. _____: Famous female general who suppressed local rebellion in Ming China.

14. _____: Ming Chinese eunuch who commanded a Chinese flotilla of ships that visited Sumatra, India, the Persian Gulf, Aden, and East Africa in the early 1400s.

15. _____: Philosophy that supported the social structure and the imperial power in China.

16. _____: Author of a new school of Confucian thought; argued that knowledge was intuitive and that thought was inseparable from action.

17. _____: Conquerors of the Ming by 1664.

Korea and Japan

18. _____: Korean dynasty established about the same time as the Ming.

19. _____: Indigenous Korean script, invented by King Sejong.

20. _____: Lands granted to *yangban* officials as payment.

21. _____: Korean armored ships.

22. _____: Best-known Korean art expression in this period.

23. _____: During his reign in Korea, it reached its height of cultural achievements, and the modern boundaries of the country were fixed; he is credited with creation of the Korean phonetic alphabet.

24. _____: Local lords in Japan who held the real reins of power since the Ashikaga shogunate.

25. _____: The finest extant example of late Warring States castle construction.

26. _____: Japanese military leader who conquered the feudal lords at home and invaded Korea.

27. _____: Founder of the Tokugawa Shogunate in 1600.

28. _____: Battle by which the Tokugawa family established their dominance in Japan for 250 years.

29. _____: Dramatic form developed in Japan in the fourteenth century, inspired by Buddhist themes.

30. _____, _____: Finest examples of Muromachi architecture.

Southeast Asia

31. _____: Great temple of the Khmer empire, it is the epitome of classical Cambodian architecture.

32. _____: Its name means "free"; it was established as an independent state under Rama Khamheng.

33. _____: The religion that came to pervade Indonesia and Malaysia in this era.

TRY THESE MULTIPLE-CHOICE QUESTIONS

1. _____Through the course of the Ming dynasty, the government (1) remained committed to outside ideas and trade; (2) began by being open to the outside but increasingly turned inward; (3) was militarily strong to the end; (4) suffered from a poor economy throughout; (5) none of the above.

2. _____The Ming emperor whose capital was at Nanjing and who restored traditional Chinese culture and reformed the laws and various aspects of government was (1) Wang Yangming; (2) Hongwu; (3) Ashikaga; (4) Sejong; (5) Shen Du.

3. _____The Ming took over from outside conquerors and were toppled by outside conquerors. These were, respectively, (1) Chin and Mongols; (2) Monguls and Manchus; (3) Mongols and Song; (4) Koreans and Manchus; (5) Manchus and Tang.

4. _____The Mongol rule in China fell because of (1) attacks from Muslims; (2) confrontation with the West; (3) an insider palace coup; (4) war with other inner Asian nomads; (5) no orderly method of succession and bureaucratic breakdown . _____

5. _____The most enduring pillar of stability in Ming government was (1) the army; (2) the navy; (3) the eunuchs; (4) the bureaucracy; (5) the church.

6. _____Ming values of balance and formalism are well represented in architecture in the design of (1) the Temple of the Golden Pavilion; (2) the Temple of the Silver Pavilion; (3) the shrine at Nikko; (4) the Forbidden City; (5) only 1 and 2 are correct.

7. _____The following were all factors in the decline of the Ming dynasty EXCEPT (1) official corruption; (2) Western attacks on Chinese ports; (3) overpopulation; (4) rebellion and piracy; (5) inflexibility in administration.

8. _____The dynasty in China overthrown by the Ming was that of the (1) Yuan; (2) Tang; (3) Qin; (4) Thai; (5) Sui.

9. _____One major characteristic of the Ming dynasty was its (1) eagerness to adopt foreign customs; (2) reluctance to revive ancient literature and art forms; (3) governmental despotism; (4) physical isolation from the rest of the world; (5) none of the above.

10. _____ Which of the following was NOT one of the *sengoku daimyo* or Warring States lords in Japan? (1) Oda Nobunaga; (2) Zeami Motokiyo; (3) Toyotomi Hideyoshi; (4) Tokugawa Ieyasu; (5) none of the above.

11. _____Under the Tokugawa Shogunate, Japan (1) expanded trade with Europe; (2) encouraged Christian missionaries to establish schools; (3) excluded all Westerners except a few Dutch traders; (4) became a dependent state of China; (5) none of the above.

12. _____The capital of the Ming dynasty beginning with Yongle was (1) Canton; (2) Beijing; (3) Shanghai; (4) Delhi; (5) Nagasaki.

13. _____The main reason given for the Ming government decision to halt overseas voyages was (1) the death of Yongle; (2) defeat in the Indian Ocean; (3) defeat in Southeast Asia; (4) they were considered to be too expensive; (5) none of the above.

14. _____The situation of women in China, Korea, and Japan was (1) similar insofar as women steadily got more rights; (2) similar in that women lost privileges they previously enjoyed; (3) different in that women were treated much better in China than in Korea and Japan; (4) different in that women were treated better in Japan than in Korea or China; (5) dependent on the influence of Legalism.

15. _____Korea and Japan were (1) different insofar as Japan was more influenced by China than was Korea; (2) similar in that both accepted Christian influences; (3) similar in that both rejected all Chinese cultural influence; (4) different in that Korea was more influenced by China than was Japan; (5) similar in that both had been conquered by China.

16. _____Which of the following is NOT TRUE of the Tokugawa era in Japan? (1) Confucian philosophy was promoted; (2) the power of the daimyo grew slowly but continuously; (3) Japan welcomed trade but not evangelism; (4) there was a hostage system to control the feudal lords; (5) the emperor's power continued to be limited.

17. _____Southeast Asia in the fourteenth through seventeenth centuries (1) was dominated by China; (2) was dominated by India; (3) was fragmented down to the village level; (4) was characterized by a succession of short-lived empires; (5) came under the control of Christian empires.

DO YOU KNOW THE SIGNIFICANCE OF THESE TERMS?

Identify each of the following terms and evaluate them in terms of their significance for world history.

Hongwu

Central Kingdom

Zhongyuan

Wang Yangming

Ming Blue

Qin Liangyu

King Sejong

Chosŏn dynasty

The Register of Licentious Women

Admiral Yi Sunsin

Hideyoshi's Edict on Changing Status

alternate attendance system

sakoku

Rama Khamheng

Kingdom of Majapahit

THE PLACE

A.   Using maps in the chapter, locate these natural boundaries and places on the map on the next page.

Irrawaddy River	Burma	Salween River	Thailand
Mekong River	Vietnam	Philippine Islands	Laos
Sumatra	China	Malaysia	Java
Mindanao	Indian Ocean	Indonesia	Pacific Ocean

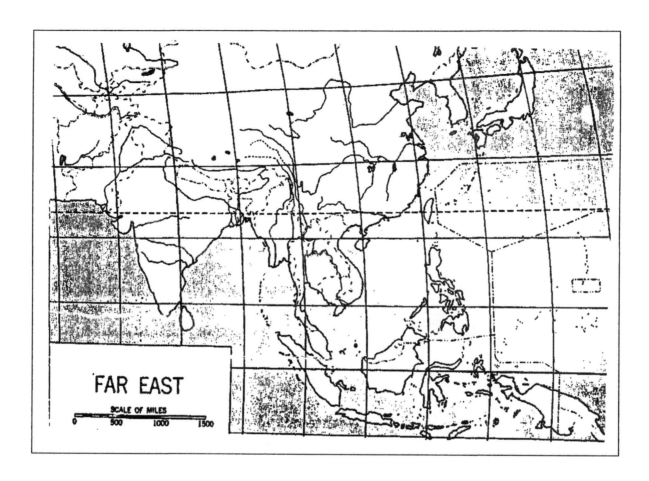

RELATIONSHIPS IN TIME

Give the dates for each dynasty and write in the one or two most important facts about each of the rulers listed under them.

Ming dynasty

Hongwu

Yongle

Chosŏn dynasty

King T'aejo

Yi Sejong

Give the dates of each of the two shogunates listed below and briefly describe their key features. Tell what each of the two intervening rulers accomplished.

Muromachi Shogunate

Nobunaga

Hideyoshi

Tokugawa Shogunate

ARRIVING AT CONCLUSIONS

Here are some quotations from scholars dealing with the significance of this period of history. Answer the accompanying questions briefly and be prepared to defend your position.

1.   "Korea's [Yi dynasty] state ostensibly dominated the society, but in practice landed aristocratic families could keep the state at bay and perpetuate their local power for centuries. This pattern persisted until the late 1940s, when landed dominance was obliterated in a northern revolution and in southern land reform; since that time the balance has shifted toward strong central power and top-down administration of the whole country in both North and South Korea. Precisely because of the tension between central power and landed wealth [Yi dynasty] leaders could achieve stability over time by playing one force off against the other. This . . . adaptable system . . . lasted five hundred years. But it was not a system that could be mobilized to keep the imperial powers at bay . . . instead it fell before them. The balance of power between monarchy and aristocracy was an asset for the maintenance of stability, but it was a liability when Korea was faced with the need to expand central power to mobilize resources for defense and development." (Bruce Cumings, *Korea's Place in the Sun* [New York: W.W. Norton, 1997], p. 73.)

Notice in this quote that the 500-year reign of the last Korean dynasty set conditions for modern Korean politics both in South Korea and communist North Korea—very different states. What type of government is favored? Are both North and South Korea moving toward that style of leadership on a permanent basis? Notice also that the quote makes the Yi system create a tradeoff between long-term domestic balance and capability to stand up to foreign challenges. Compare that assessment with the old system in China.

2.   "It was a peasant rebellion that ultimately dismembered the Yuan. In revolt equally against the harsh exploitation of a ruthless landlord class and the oppression of a foreign Mongol regime, the common people were inspired by doctrines of secret societies which promised them deliverance from the suffering of the traditional order. These organizations . . . existed deep within the body of peasant society and they harbored values and beliefs strikingly at odds with the high culture of the Chinese elite classes, the ideology of the Confucian state. . . .

"Chu Yuan-chang (1328–98), the founder of the Ming empire, started his career as a member of one of the rebel bands. . . . Motivated in part by a strong hatred of the landlord class and ever mindful of his own experience of poverty, Chu took stern measures to prevent his soldiers from harming the common people. Partly because of this . . . Chu was able to eliminate competing Chinese leaders. . . . Initially, he maintained his allegiance to the secret society elements. . . . At the same time he set about building an administrative apparatus of scholars, gentry members and former Yuan civil servants. By 1367, when he sent his armies north to sweep the Mongol remnants from China, he was ready to disavow his connections with the secret societies and put himself forward as a champion of orthodoxy qualified to take the Chinese throne. In 1368 he became the first emperor of the Ming dynasty. . . .

"Once in power Chu devoted his energies to the task of reuniting the Chinese into a single state. Faced with the problem of holding power and building an administration, the Ming founder soon forgot the radical ideals of the peasant movement in favor of an orthodox Confucianism. Thus did potential social revolution turn to cultural conservatism once power was attained." (Edward L. Farmer et al., *Comparative History of Civilizations in Asia*, Vol. 1 [Reading, MA: Addison-Wesley, 1977], pp. 444–45.)

Did Chu Yuan-chang have to cast off his radical background and embrace the tried-and-true Confucian orthodoxy in order to successfully establish a dynasty? Is it easier to attack and topple a foreign regime than it is to change the underlying policies of government?

QUESTIONS TO THINK ABOUT

1.   Evaluate the advantages and disadvantages to China of its civil service examinations.

2.   How was Japanese feudalism different from and similar to European feudalism? Were Japanese and European attitudes toward trade similar?

3.   Why did both China and Japan eventually try to isolate themselves from cultural contacts with the West? Why did Korea follow suit?

4.   How has the history of east Asia during the period 1300–1650 affected the area in the twenty-first century? Use specific examples to illustrate key points in your response.

CHAPTER 14

European Cultural and Religious Transformations: The Renaissance and the Reformation 1300–1600

The Renaissance was a "golden age" in Europe reminiscent of other eras in other civilizations that set the standards for excellence in culture. The Reformation was a great religious reform movement that shook the foundations of society and religion. Unlike some epochs of outstanding achievement, both came on the heels of a period of crisis in Europe characterized by war, famine, plague, and economic hard times, and both movements would bring sweeping changes to Europe, changes that would have dramatic implications for the entire world.

The period known as the Renaissance in Europe was not the first time that the people of Europe recovered from a prolonged political, economic, and cultural decline. During the Carolingian era, a new civilization emerged out of the wreckage of the Roman Empire in the West. Sufficient peace was established to permit the revival of art and scholarship in the monasteries. After the collapse of the Carolingian Empire and a relapse into barbarism, European civilization experienced another rebirth, which has been called the Renaissance of the twelfth century. So profoundly were all facets of life revitalized, from agriculture to theology, during that period that we have been obliged to reconsider the crucial importance of the Renaissance that took place in Europe between 1300 and 1600.

In the past, the Middle Ages were often described as a period of barbaric manners and religious superstition or fanaticism, and scholars viewed the Renaissance as a sharp break from the medieval world. Today we recognize not only the heights attained by medieval men and women but also the substantial continuity of development from medieval to early modern civilization. Thus, the Renaissance should properly be observed as a period of cultural transition—a bridge between medieval culture and modern times. Nevertheless, the exceptional accomplishments of Renaissance artists and intellectuals serve as evidence of the period's fertile creative environment, making it a unique and fascinating chapter in the history of Western civilization.

To understand the Reformation, we must stretch our historical imagination to encompass a broad range of human motives. In this period we find passionate conflict among such religious zealots as Luther, Calvin, and Loyola over points of doctrine, such as the presence of Christ in Holy Communion. A modern observer might ask why the protagonists could not simply agree to disagree and allow persons to believe as they saw best. To answer that question, we must put ourselves into the minds of sixteenth-century men and women who assumed that religion was the ultimate service that God required of human beings and that only the Christian religion was true and pleasing to God. In such a climate, religious controversy was certain to become bitter, and it should not be surprising that religious discord could so often turn violent.

The passion that fueled religious conflict, however, also stimulated remarkable achievements of the human spirit. Martin Luther's German translation of the Bible, for example, a work of extraordinary poetic and religious power, has profoundly shaped German culture. A more gracious if less intense passion also inspired the composition of *The Book of Common Prayer* by the Christian humanist Archbishop of Canterbury, Thomas Cranmer. This masterpiece, like the works of Shakespeare, has exercised a strong and lasting influence on the development of English language and thought.

YOU SHOULD HAVE A BASIC UNDERSTANDING OF:

The Italian Renaissance—leading painters, sculptors, and architects along with their patrons.

The Northern Renaissance—how printing spurred it on and who its key writers and painters were.

The Protestant Reformation, with emphasis on its roots, Luther's role, and the ways it spread over Europe.

Reformation in England and the rise of Anglicanism.

The reforms of Zwingli and Calvin.

The efforts Catholics made toward correcting the abuses that had crept into the Church.

HAVE YOU MASTERED THE BASIC FACTS?

Fill in each of the following blanks with the correct identification.

Humanism and the Italian Renaissance

1. _____: "Father of humanism" and a transitional figure between the Renaissance and the Middle Ages.

2. _____: Disaster that formed the backdrop for the stories of the *Decameron*.

3. _____: Important early humanist and author of the *Decameron*.

4. _____: Intellectual movement beginning in fourteenth-century Italy that stressed classical learning and individualism.

5. _____: Italian term for the fourteenth century, often used to designate a leading Renaissance era.

6. _____ and _____: Two ancient Greek philosophers who wielded a great deal of influence during the Renaissance.

7. _____: Florentine artist with a sensitive style that emphasized line, well exemplified in his *Birth of Venus*.

8. _____: Most illustrious Renaissance sculptor; also a painter (the Sistine Chapel) and architect (St. Peter's dome).

9. _____: Genius of many talents, famous primarily as the painter of such masterpieces as *The Last Supper* and the *Mona Lisa*; notable also as a student of physics, anatomy, and other sciences.

10. _____: A style in late sixteenth-century Italian art, reflecting the stresses of the age, that evoked shock in the viewer.

The Northern Renaissance

11. _____: Author of *The Praise of Folly* and the most influential of the northern humanists.

12. _____: This famous book, best known of Sir Thomas More's writings, described life in an ideal state.

13. _____: French skeptic who developed the literary form of the essay.

14. _____: *King Lear, Hamlet,* and *A Midsummer Night's Dream* all came from the pen of this most famous of all English playwrights.

15. _____: Writing about life from "the sewers to the heavens," this French humanist created the fictional characters of Gargantua and Pantagruel.

16. _____: Nuremberg painter whose work was a blend of both medieval and Renaissance themes; best known for his engravings and woodcuts.

17. _____: Author of *Don Quixote,* the best-known literary work of the Spanish Renaissance.

18. _____: Flemish painter who perfected the technique of oil painting, enabling him to paint with greater realism and attention to detail.

19. _____: German printer who introduced the use of movable type to Europe.

Crisis in the Catholic Church; Luther and the Protestant Reformation

20. _____: Pope whose confrontation with Philip IV of France led to humiliation for the papacy.

21. _____: Prague minister who taught that the church was composed of a universal priesthood of believers.

22. _____: Term used to refer to the split between the papacy in Rome and the papacy in Avignon.

23. _____: Political unit including all German states during the early sixteenth century.

24. _____: Papal agent whose activities in Germany for raising money to aid in the construction of St. Peter's Basilica in Rome aroused the ire of Martin Luther.

25. _____: Luther's answer to the problem of eternal salvation.

26. _____: Pope who called upon Luther to recant and return to orthodoxy.

27. _____: Holy Roman Emperor during the time of Luther's break with the church.

28. _____: Imperial assembly before which Luther appeared in 1519 to defend himself against the charge of heresy.

29. _____: Fourteenth-century English theologian who advanced many of the theories espoused more than a century later by Martin Luther.

30. _____: Promises to remit part or all of the penalty to be paid after death for one's sins, the sale of which angered Martin Luther.

31. _____: Series of propositions on which Luther called for debate, thereby unwittingly setting in motion the Reformation.

32. _____: Agreement (1555) by which Lutheranism received legal recognition; it provided that the prince of each state should decide whether his subjects were to be Lutheran or Catholic.

33. _____: English Tudor king who eliminated papal authority over the English church.

34. _____: Swiss patriot who led the Protestant revolt in Switzerland until his death in a civil war.

35. _____: Author of the influential *Institutes of the Christian Religion.*

36. _____: Evangelical sect centered in Germany and the Netherlands whose members believed that adults alone should be baptized.

37. _____: English monarch who temporarily reinstated Catholicism.

38. _____: French Calvinists.

The Catholic Counter-Reformation

39. _____: Council at which the Catholic Church codified its reaction to the Protestant Reformation.

40. _____: Founder of the Society of Jesus (Jesuits), an order that combated the spread of Protestantism and returned many to Catholicism.

41. _____: Dominican friar and mystic who ruled Florence for four years as a fanatical reformer before he was deposed and executed.

42. _____: Founder of the order of Carmelites, this Spanish nun was famous for her written accounts of her mystical experiences.

43. _____: Reforming pope of the Catholic Reformation who labored to correct church abuses and restore integrity to the papacy.

TRY THESE MULTIPLE-CHOICE QUESTIONS

1. _____ The Renaissance included all of the following characteristics EXCEPT (1) an intense renewal of interest in the literature of classical Greece and Rome; (2) a lessening of interest in the world outside Europe because of increased attention to the development of new art forms; (3) a stimulation of artists through the imitation of classical art forms; (4) an increased emphasis on individualism and skepticism; (5) a renewed interest and concern for affairs of the secular world.

2.   _____ In general, it can be said that the Renaissance (1) marked a sudden departure from the culture of the Middle Ages; (2) placed great stress on otherworldliness and asceticism; (3) led to an individualism so strong that its excesses brought social amorality and lawlessness; (4) all of the above; (5) none of the above.

3.   _____ Renaissance artists found their patrons (1) in the papacy; (2) among the wealthy bankers; (3) among the princes and despots of the city-states; (4) among merchant capitalists; (5) all of the above.

4.   _____ The Latin writer most praised by humanist scholars was (1) Cicero; (2) Juvenal; (3) Livy; (4) Virgil; (5) Marcus Aurelius.

5.   _____ Choose the number at the end of this question that gives the correct comparisons between humanism and scholasticism. (a) Humanism placed greater emphasis on art and literature in education, while the scholastics stressed the sciences and professional training. (b) Both humanism and scholasticism venerated the classical heritage. (c) Scholastics regarded themselves as superior to the ancients, while the humanists saw themselves as distinctly inferior. (d) Humanists displayed little interest in old manuscripts, while scholastics continued their active study and appreciation of them. (1) only d; (2) b and c; (3) a and b; (4) only b; (5) only c.

6.   _____ Humanist scholars tended to (1) be highly creative and original; (2) disparage the achievements of the Middle Ages; (3) be recipients of governmental, academic and tutorial positions provided by wealthy patrons because of renewed emphasis on literature and the arts; (4) represent a "new birth" of classical values; (5) all of the above.

7.   _____ Which of the following was NOT a leading sculptor of the Renaissance? (1) Donatello; (2) Verrocchio; (3) Michelangelo; (4) Gutenberg; (5) Ghiberti.

8.   _____ The term LEAST applicable to the typical Renaissance humanist would be (1) individualistic; (2) critical; (3) atheistic; (4) imitative; (5) citizen of the world.

9.   _____ A label that might be applied with some accuracy to Sir Thomas More would be (1) atheist; (2) capitalist; (3) socialist; (4) individualist; (5) none of the above.

10.   _____ The Northern Renaissance differed from that of the south by (1) coming later in time; (2) placing greater reliance on kings as patrons of the arts; (3) making greater utilization of the printing press in the diffusion of knowledge; (4) placing greater emphasis on social reform; (5) all of the above.

11.   _____ Unlike literary figures of the Italian Renaissance, those of the north were more likely to (1) be sharply critical of contemporary social ills; (2) ignore the church and churchmen; (3) have a romantic, otherworldly attitude; (4) all of the above; (5) none of the above.

12.   _____ In general, Renaissance people differed from the people of the Middle Ages in their (1) greater sense of community and lessened sense of individualism; (2) more secular outlook; (3) lack of interest in scholarship; (4) more serious interest in divine matters; (5) more religious outlook.

13.   _____ A serious, although satirical, attack on human frailties is to be found in (1) *The Faerie Queene*; (2) *Doctor Faustus*; (3) *Ascent of Mount Ventoux*; (4) *In Praise of Folly*; (5) *The Decameron*.

14. _____ A central theme of *Don Quixote de la Mancha* is (1) the importance of preserving the best of medieval culture as the peoples of Europe entered the modern era; (2) a critical examination of the major tenets of the Christian religion; (3) showing the anachronistic nature of the chivalric code in a changing world; (4) encouraging the spread of Lutheranism; (5) reinforcing the values of the Spanish monarchy.

15. _____ The High Renaissance in Italy was characterized by all of the following EXCEPT (1) a shift in the focus of artistic activity from Florence to Rome and Venice; (2) a decline in the interest of the papacy in sponsoring artistic endeavors; (3) great achievements in architecture; (4) increased attention of painters to the central theme of a picture and less attention to color, movement, and details; (5) the use of art to make a statement.

16. _____ The queen whose court served as the center of artistic and intellectual life during the Renaissance in England was (1) Isabella; (2) Elizabeth; (3) Irene; (4) Theodora; (5) Hildegard.

17. _____ *The Prince* (1513) is (1) a secular, realistic treatise on politics by Machiavelli; (2) a play by Shakespeare; (3) a book of moral instruction for a Christian ruler by Erasmus; (4) a collection of orations by Cicero discovered by Italian humanists; (5) a religious treatise by Luther.

18. _____ By the early seventeenth century, all of the following were largely Protestant EXCEPT (1) Prussia; (2) Spain; (3) Scotland; (4) Sweden; (5) England.

19. _____ Ulrich Zwingli agreed with Luther on all of the following EXCEPT this issue: (1) justification by faith; (2) the interpretation of the meaning of baptism and communion; (3) the supremacy of scriptural authority over papal authority; (4) criticism of monasticism and clerical celibacy; (5) Zwingli advocated additional grounds for divorce.

20. _____ Which of the following occurred FIRST? (1) Henry VIII's marriage to Anne Boleyn; (2) the execution of Sir Thomas More; (3) Queen Mary's restoration of Catholicism; (4) Parliament's completion of seizing church lands; (5) publication of the English Bible.

21. _____ A direct stimulus to Luther's call for debate on his Ninety-Five Theses was (1) a debate with John Eck on the question of papal infallibility; (2) the sale of indulgences by Tetzel; (3) his desire to defy his sentence of excommunication; (4) the Augsburg Confession; (5) none of the above.

22. _____ The strongest centers of Huguenot activity in the sixteenth century were to be found in (1) France; (2) Italy; (3) Portugal; (4) Ireland; (5) England.

23. _____ The doctrine of the justification by faith is most closely associated with (1) Calvin; (2) Knox; (3) Luther; (4) Zwingli; (5) Cranmer.

24. _____ After Luther was declared an outlaw and heretic, he was protected by (1) the Holy Roman Emperor; (2) the bishop of Mainz; (3) the elector of Saxony; (4) Henry VIII of England; (5) Charles V.

25. _____ The early Reformation in England differed from the early Reformation in Germany most significantly in the (1) absence of economic factors; (2) lack of doctrinal differences with Rome; (3) absence of political factors; (4) reluctance of the leaders to form a new church; (5) concern over investiture.

26. _____ Choose the number at the end of this question that gives the correct generalizations about Luther and Calvin. (a) Calvin placed stronger emphasis on loyalty to the state than did Luther. (b) Luther's central doctrine was the sovereignty of God, while Calvin stressed grace and forgiveness. (c) Calvin's belief in the omnipotence and omniscience of God led to a belief in predestination. (d) Like Calvin, Luther rejected all of the sacraments of the Catholic Church. (1) only c; (2) a and b; (3) only d; (4) b, c, and d; (5) only a is correct.

27. _____ The Council of Trent (1) reaffirmed the role of the seven sacraments; (2) approved the continuation of indulgences, pilgrimages, the veneration of relics, and the cult of the Virgin; (3) strengthened the papacy; (4) included the necessity of good works as well as grace for salvation; (5) all of the above.

28. _____ Henry VIII obtained support in his campaign to control the church in England from (1) More; (2) Cranmer; (3) Charles V; (4) Mary Stuart; (5) none of the above.

29. _____ In which of the following areas did the Reformation occur LAST? (1) Germany; (2) England; (3) Switzerland; (4) Scotland; (5) Holland.

30. _____ The Reformation resulted in all of the following EXCEPT (1) a reduction in the authority of the king and an increase in the power of the nobility in almost all strongly Catholic countries; (2) continued religious intolerance and persecution in much of Europe; (3) permanent divisions in Western Christendom; (4) renewed interest in education; (5) councils of mediation between Protestants and Catholics.

31. _____ The medieval ideal of the political unity of Christendom was destroyed by the evolution of the (1) universal church; (2) nation-state; (3) rise of political democracy; (4) influence of scholasticism; (5) all of the above.

FOCUSING ON MAJOR TOPICS

Although they shared many of the same classical sources, the medieval scholastics differed from the Renaissance humanists. In the blank before each of the following items, write an S to indicate a characteristic of the scholastics or an H to indicate a humanist attitude.

1. _____ Truth comes ultimately from God.

2. _____ Placed particular emphasis on the works of Plato.

3. _____ Their name was derived from a Latin term, which Roman authors applied to a liberal or literary education.

4. _____ Emphasized the sciences and the professions—law, medicine, and theology.

5. _____ Centered their attention on Aristotle's scientific writings, as well as other classical works on astronomy, medicine, and mathematics.

6. _____ Stressed history, grammar, rhetoric, poetry, and moral philosophy.

7. _____ Disdained the sciences.

8. _____ Always felt inferior to the ancients.

9. _____ Saw themselves as equal to the classical writers.

10. _____ Recovery of Greek and Roman learning was a consuming passion.

11. _____ The world of here and now holds delights that should not be shunned.

12. _____ Stressed the freedom and dignity of the individual.

13. _____ Tried to synthesize Christianity and Plato.

14. _____ Tried to synthesize Christianity and Aristotle.

Here are three giants of the Renaissance. Give a brief sketch of each, identifying his field of work and general accomplishments, and explain how each was representative of certain facets of Renaissance culture.

Michelangelo   Erasmus   Shakespeare

RELATIONSHIPS IN TIME

Place the following names and events in the correct column and century below. If a life spanned more than one century, write the name of the century in which the person died.

Petrarch
Bramante
Josquin des Prés
Medici family ruled Florence
Botticelli
Brueghel the Elder
Erasmus
Leonardo da Vinci
Boccaccio
Shakespeare
Holbein the Younger
Giotto
Michelangelo

Sir Thomas More
Raphael
Brunelleschi
Montaigne
Jan van Eyck
Giorgione
Donatello
Ghiberti
Titian
Ulrich von Hutten
Dürer
Gutenberg's Bible
Cervantes

Italian Renaissance   **Northern Renaissance**

1300

1400

1500

1600

Within each group, number the items in chronological order.

The Protestant Reformation in Germany

1. _____ Peasants' revolt

2. _____ Peace of Augsburg

3. _____ Augsburg Confession

4. _____ Luther's call for debate on his Ninety-Five Theses

The Protestant Revolt in England

1. _____ The reign of Elizabeth I

2. _____ Henry VIII breaks with Rome

3. _____ Reign of Catholic Mary Tudor

4. _____ Cranmer legalized Henry VIII's union with Anne Boleyn

The Catholic Counter-Reformation

1. _____ Jesuit order founded

2. _____ Council of Trent ends

3. _____ Savonarola becomes ruler of Florence

4. _____ Cardinal Ximenes dies

5. _____ Paul III reigns as pope

Here is a date you need to know: Luther issued his call for debate on his Ninety-Five Theses in _____. Why is this date important? It is also the same year that Cardinal Ximenes died. What did he do?

Martin Luther and Ulrich Zwingli were almost the same age. What similarities and differences were there between the activities of the two men?

Henry VIII and John Calvin were the same age. How were they alike, and how were they different?

DO YOU KNOW THE SIGNIFICANCE OF THESE TERMS?

In the space provided, identify each of the following terms and evaluate them with regard to their significance for world history.

"just price"

Christine de Pizan

Divine Comedy

The Prince

Petrarch

Giotto

quattrocento

La Giaconda

The Lagoon of Venice Map

Erasmus

Don Quixote

Augsburg Confession

Anne Ayscough

Huguenots

Council of Trent

ARRIVING AT CONCLUSIONS

Here are some quotations from scholars dealing with the significance of this period of history. Answer the accompanying questions briefly, and be prepared to defend your position.

1.   "If humanists in general adhered to no peculiar ideology, their special interests—language and history—led them to understand the world in terms different from those of their chief intellectual rivals, the scholastic philosophers and theologians. The humanists found meaning in neither the abstract syntheses nor the petty logical quarrels of the scholastics, but rather in practical matters of politics and morality and . . . in the unique and particular elements of literature and history. The humanists therefore approached the New Testament, among other things, with different purposes in mind than the scholastics. The humanists' interests lay not in the construction of a comprehensive theological system that answered all possible questions bearing on salvation, and that did so with logical rigor worthy of an Aristotle. They valued the New Testament instead as the source of pure moral and religious doctrine and as the record of early Christian experience." (Jerry H. Bentley, *Humanists and Holy Writ* [Princeton, NJ: Princeton University Press, 1983], p. 8.)

What did scholastics think was the source of pure moral and religious doctrine? What was the practical importance of the above conflict between humanists and scholastics? The humanists to whom Bentley refers were Erasmus and similar scholars outside Italy. How did their interests differ from those of Italian humanists?

2. "From one point of view Renaissance man was a highly sophisticated creature—skeptical, linguistically subtle, aware of a great variety of views and ways of expressing these views. From another point of view, he now seems amazingly quaint and simpleminded. He still held to the traditional cosmology and physics, and to the traditional physiology and psychology as well. He not only believed the earth to be motionless and the stars made of a translucent nothingness, but he believed in the four elements and the four 'humours,' blood, choler, phlegm, and melancholy, the mixture of which in the body determined temperament or personality. He believed, further, that there were correspondences between the macrocosm of physical nature and the microcosm of the human soul, so that emeralds protected virginity, for example, and the rumble in the bowels related to the thunder in the sky." (Roland N. Stromberg, *An Intellectual History of Modern Europe* [New York: Appleton-Century-Crofts, 1966], p. 17.)

How does this passage help support the view that the Renaissance was a time of transition? What evidence from Chapter 14 also indicates that Western civilization evolved unevenly during the Renaissance? Can you find instances of "cultural lag" in the modern world, for example, in the horoscope columns of daily newspapers?

3. "The stage on which the Renaissance woman lived is often bathed in the luminous nostalgic glow of a 'Golden Age.' It was a Golden Age for a few women, very few, and the light was less a broad glow than a spotlight. . . . The poetry and letters of devout, learned Vittoria Colonna to Pietro Bembo, to Castiglione, and most famously the sonnets and letters she exchanged with Michelangelo, who wrote a moving poem on her death, still sound for us from yellowed pages. . . . But there must have been many gifted girls lost in anonymity. Large, busy ateliers like those of . . . the Bellini in Padua quite possibly put their daughters to work with the boy apprentices. Who knows what telling passages in which paintings may have been theirs? . . . Careers open to women were the three perennials: housewifery and childbearing, the religious life, and whoredom." (Kate Simon, *A Renaissance Tapestry* [New York: Harper & Row, 1988], pp. 139–41.)

In light of this passage, how shall we interpret Renaissance culture's strong value of developing the potential of the individual? In addition to women, were other social groups overlooked by the Renaissance ideal of cultivating well-rounded individuals? Who were the patrons of the great artists and intellectuals of the period, and to what extent did their values affect the role of women and other social groups?

4. History suggests that unforeseen results often stem from major changes in society. The Reformation offers ample evidence to support this generalization.

    "The religious upheaval produced some outcomes that were inconsistent with others. Certain Protestant communities seemed to contribute to the growth of the democratic spirit; others, as in the case of Prussia, were on the side of monarchical absolutism. In some cases religious change led quickly to toleration, in others, to savage intolerance. Men were exiled or burned for their faith by Catholic and Protestant alike. Witch hunting grew throughout the sixteenth century until it actually reached its hysterical climax in the seventeenth. Its victims must be numbered in the thousands. Protestantism may have contributed to the liberation of the spirit of man; but in attacking the ceremonials and 'superstitions' of Catholicism it in many cases destroyed artistic works of inestimable value. . . . Opinions will differ as to the ultimate significance of this fateful age. No Catholic can contemplate without regret the tremendous breach in the structure of his church; no Protestant can look without deep feeling at the founding years of his faith." (Ernest John Knapton, *Europe, 1450–1815* [New York: Charles Scribner's Sons, 1958], p. 229.)

Why is it so difficult to reach conclusions about the significance of the Reformation for Western civilization? What generalizations are you willing to make about the heritage of the Reformation? It has been said that history reveals few black and white lessons in human affairs, but mostly shades of gray. How does the history of the Reformation support this generalization?

5. Lewis Spitz represents the viewpoint of many historians that the Protestant Reformation generally favored the growth of political liberty and limited constitutional government.

> "Perhaps the greatest political contribution of the reformers to political thought may have been an element of stability derived from their theocentric orientation. They had a way of putting earthly potentates into perspective. In the final edition of Calvin's *Institutes* he wrote . . . : 'And that our hearts may not fail us, Paul stimulates us with another consideration—that Christ has redeemed us at the immense price which our redemption cost him, that we may not be submissive to the corrupt desires of men, much less be slaves to their impiety.' . . . For the wars of religion, for independence and the age of the great revolutions to come, the type of inner-directed citizen rather than mere subject constituted the solid core of modern political progress. 'On their feet before God, on their knees before men; on their knees before God, on their feet before men' is an old saying not without relevance in early modern times." (Lewis W. Spitz, *The Protestant Reformation, 1517–1559* [New York: Harper & Row, 1985], p. 365.)

Compare Spitz's point of view with that expressed in the text. How are they alike, and how do they differ? Argue for or against Spitz's contention that the Protestant Reformation tended to develop inner-directed citizens.

QUESTIONS TO THINK ABOUT

1. Why was humanism in its broadest sense a revolt from the religious emphasis of the Middle Ages?

2. What aspects of medieval culture would you defend against the sweeping criticism of the humanists? What were some of the negative qualities of humanism?

3. How would you explain the fact that the Renaissance began in Italy almost two centuries before it spread to northern Europe?

4. In what ways did Renaissance art and literature reflect the material conditions of the age?

5. How did the Renaissance courtier differ from the medieval knight?

6. How would you interpret the phrase, "The oil of commerce in Italy lighted the lamp of culture"?

7. List as many characteristics as possible that distinguish Renaissance from medieval art.

8. Do you think that churches—in their organization, objectives, and general philosophy—reflect trends in our changing society, or do they tend to exist distinct and separate from the times? If you think that churches *do* reflect existing times, in what ways will they be likely to change with the times, and in what areas will there be strong resistance to modification?

9. Some scholars contend that the Reformation was only one aspect of a more general collapse of the unity of life in the Middle Ages. What evidence can you cite to either support or refute this interpretation?

10. Can you argue that the basic philosophy of Luther was really the religious manifestation of Renaissance individualism?

11. Can you find in modern institutions any examples of culture lag comparable to the failure of the medieval church to keep pace with the new demands of the Renaissance era? If so, in what way does your study of cause and effect in the religious revolt illuminate the modern religious situation?

12. It is sometimes said that the Reformation marked a permanent division of Christianity. To what extent is this true? Was there a single church in 1520? Explain. What evidence is there today of serious efforts to restore unity to Christendom?

CHAPTER 15

State Development in Europe: Western and Central Europe, Russia, and the Balkans to 1650

The nation-state in Europe developed steadily during the period 1300–1650 as European monarchies consolidated their control and political institutions matured out of the Middle Ages, the Renaissance, and the Reformation. They were shaped by a dramatic combination of forces that included wars, famines, plagues, intellectual and religious change, and economic revolution. From England to Russia, these countries took their own unique paths to nationhood as they worked out the development of national states. Certainly, the states of Europe demonstrated remarkable development in the period 1500–1650.

By the mid-seventeenth century, leading nation-states in Europe already demonstrated many of the characteristics we have come to associate with the modern nation: well-defined boundaries, diverse populations, standing armies, bureaucracies, and developing economies driven by strong national interests. In the process, the leaders of these developing states were caught up in often dramatic rivalries and confrontations that would affect not only Europe but the world as well.

YOU SHOULD HAVE A BASIC UNDERSTANDING OF:

Western and Central Europe, 1300–1500.

Politics, diplomacy, and religious wars, 1556–1598.

The Thirty Years' War.

Russia: From the Mongols to the Romanovs.

The Balkans: Byzantine collapse and Ottoman rule.

HAVE YOU MASTERED THE BASIC FACTS?

Fill in each of the following blanks with the correct identification.

Western and Central Europe, 1300–1500

1. _____: Weapon that gave English armies an advantage over their French opponents during the Hundred Years' War, until the French adopted the use of gunpowder.

2. _____: Peasant girl who stimulated French patriotism against the English during the Hundred Years' War.

3. _____: Series of thirty years of wars in England, which brought the Tudor family to power.

4. _____ : French king, one of the "new monarchs," he was called the "spider king"; he worked to replace the feudal system.

5. _____ : Special Roman Catholic court directed to seek out and punish heretics, people who believed in doctrines other than what was taught by the Church.

6. _____ : Section of Spain in which Muslim control was ended by the end of the fifteenth century.

7. _____ : Title given by the pope to Ferdinand and Isabella.

8. _____ : Ruling dynasty that won the crown of the Holy Roman Empire late in the thirteenth century and held it for centuries almost without interruption.

9. _____ : This document in 1356 provided a system for choosing the emperor in the Holy Roman Empire.

10. _____ : Commercial league of mostly German cities extending from the English Channel to the eastern end of the Baltic Sea, active between the thirteenth and seventeenth centuries.

11. _____ : Mercenary forces in Italy used by competing city-states in Italy in intra-city conflicts

12. _____ : Habsburg monarch who in the sixteenth century led European efforts to protect Catholic orthodoxy, often with military force.

13. _____ : Hungarian king from the fifteenth century who established close ties with Renaissance cities; known as a "Renaissance man," he was a patron of the arts and one of the pioneers in introducing printing to Central and Eastern Europe.

Politics, Diplomacy, and Religious Wars, 1556–1598

14. _____ : Leader of the Dutch revolt against the Spanish.

15. _____ : Popular name for the special tribunal set up by the duke of Alba in the Netherlands to stamp out treason and heresy.

16. _____ : Murder of some 10,000 Huguenots in Paris in 1572, the result of a Guise plot in which Catherine de Medici participated.

17. _____ : Catholic queen of Scotland who was the center of Catholic schemes against Elizabeth of England.

18. _____ : Leader of the revolt against Queen Mary Stuart that established the Presbyterian Church in Scotland.

19. _____ : Fleet of Spanish ships launched in 1588 and driven back by the "Protestant wind."

20. _____ : Location of major naval battle in 1571 in which the Holy League defeated the Turkish navy and after which the Ottoman navy ceased to be a threat.

Thirty Years' War

21. _____ : Incident in 1618 that involved Bohemian leaders throwing two Catholic government officials out a window in a highly charged religious atmosphere.

22. _____ : King of Sweden, monarch of the leading Lutheran power during the Thirty Years' War.

23. _____ : Son of a German innkeeper who was left an orphan and carried away by soldiers in the Thirty Years' War; he recorded his memories of the horrors of the war.

24. _____ : Order issued by Henry IV, intended to protect the liberties of French Huguenots.

25. _____ : Treaty in 1648 that confirmed the new European state system based largely on defensive alliances.

Russia: From the Mongols to the Romanovs

26. _____ : Russian city called "the Third Rome."

27. _____ : The first Russian leader to adopt the title *Tsar*; he began the process of building the modern Russian state.

28. _____ : Expanded site of the original fortress in Moscow constructed by Italian architects and technicians in the fifteenth century.

The Balkans: Byzantine Collapse and Ottoman Rule

29. _____ : Final dynasty of the Byzantine Empire.

30. _____ : Year in which the Ottomans took Constantinople.

31. _____ : Site of the siege of Vienna in 1683 resulting in the defeat of the Ottomans and the beginning of their long decline.

TRY THESE MULTIPLE-CHOICE QUESTIONS

1. _____ Factors behind the Hundred Years' War between France and England included (1) economic rivalry in Flanders; (2) a fundamental conflict of interests between the French kings and the English kings; (3) a dispute over the succession to the French throne in the fourteenth century; (4) an English claim to French territory; (5) all of the above.

2. _____ For most of the sixteenth century, the most powerful nation in Europe was (1) England; (2) Germany; (3) Denmark; (4) Spain; (5) France.

3. _____ Basic goals sought by Philip II of Spain included all of the following EXCEPT (1) the establishment of royal absolutism in all his possessions; (2) the achievement of a military alliance with the Turkish empire; (3) elimination of heresy and the strengthening of Catholicism; (4) extension of Spanish influence in Europe and overseas; (5) none of the above.

4. _____ Queen Elizabeth executed Queen Mary Stuart on charges of (1) conspiring against the English throne; (2) murdering her husband; (3) planning to marry the king of France; (4) adultery; (5) advancing the Protestant religion.

5. _____ The first arena of battle in the Thirty Years' War was (1) Bohemia; (2) Denmark; (3) Ireland; (4) Italy; (5) Hungary.

6. _____ The defeat of the Spanish Armada meant that (1) England would remain Protestant; (2) the Dutch rebellion against Spain would eventually succeed; (3) Spain suffered a costly setback; (4) all of the above; (5) none of the above.

7. _____ The French royal advisor who led France into the Thirty Years' War on the side of the Protestants was (1) Turenne; (2) Sully; (3) Richelieu; (4) Mazarin; (5) Catherine de Medici.

8. _____ The Protestant victory in 1632 during which the Swedish king, Gustavus Adolphus, was killed was (1) Lepanto; (2) White Mountain; (3) Lützen; (4) Kosovo; (5) none of the above.

9. _____ The Peace of Westphalia provided all of the following EXCEPT (1) recognition of the political fragmentation of Germany; (2) strict limitations on the authority of nation-states; (3) territorial gains for France and Sweden; (4) recognition of the independence of the Netherlands; (5) confirmation of German religious autonomy.

10. _____ Which of the following occurred FIRST? (1) defeat of the Spanish Armada; (2) completion of the Peace of Westphalia; (3) proclamation of the Edict of Nantes; (4) independence of the Netherlands; (5) Peace of Prague.

11. _____ Russian tsar in the sixteenth century who responded to those who opposed him with a cruelty consistent with his nickname, "the Terrible.": (1) Michael Romanov; (2) Boris Godunov; (3) Fedor; (4) Ivan III; (5) Ivan IV.

12. _____ Russian special forces, masked men, dressed in black, who cruelly worked to eliminate opponents to the tsar: (1) boyars; (2) zemskis; (3) cadets; (4) *oprichniki*; (5) none of the above.

13. _____ All of the following were one of the vassal states of the Ottomans EXCEPT (1) Moldavia; (2) Wallachia; (3) Transylvania; (4) Ragusa-Dubrovnik; (5) Austria.

FOCUSING ON MAJOR TOPICS

Fill in the blanks in the following narrative.

The preeminence of Spanish power and its decline in Europe is a constant theme in the period between 1560 and 1660. Intertwined with Spain's predominance was that of its ruling family, the (1) _____. In 1556, Charles V retired to a monastery, turning over his holdings in Austria and the Holy Roman Empire to his brother (2) _____. Spain, Naples and Sicily, and the Netherlands went to Charles's son, (3) _____.

Even though it seemed that Philip II had everything going for him, Spanish power began to wane in spite of some early successes. The Ottoman fleet in the Mediterranean was destroyed at the battle of (4) _____ in 1571. In his relations with the northern provinces, Philip II was less successful. Open revolt broke out in the Netherlands, led by (5) _____ "the Silent." In 1581, the Dutch United Provinces declared their (6) _____, but it was not formally recognized until the end of the Thirty Years' War in 1648.

150

Culminating years of sparring between the Catholic Philip II of Spain and the Protestant queen of England, (7) _____, Spain suffered a crushing defeat in an attempt to invade England. A huge fleet of ships, called the (8) _____, entered the English Channel in the year (9) _____, only to be driven off by the swift English ships and the famous "Protestant wind."

DO YOU KNOW THE SIGNIFICANCE OF THESE TERMS?

The following terms are representative of major trends and themes of the period. Please identify each of them and assess the terms as representative of major developments in world history.

Joan of Arc

Wars of the Roses

Reconquista

Liberum Veto

Philip II

Henry VIII

Elizabeth I

Puritans

Simplicissimus

defenstration of Prague

Zemski Sobor

Tatar Yoke

millet system

Fall of Constantinople

THE PLACE

A.   *On the outline map below, indicate by a heavy line the boundaries of the Holy Roman Empire in 1648.*

B.   *Indicate with \\\\\\ the area ruled by the Austrian Habsburgs.*

C.   *Indicate with ////// the area ruled by the Spanish Habsburgs.*

D.   *Indicate with different colors the areas that were predominately Anglican, Calvinist, Greek Orthodox, Islamic, Lutheran, and Roman Catholic.*

E.   *Locate each of the following items on the outline map using the maps in the textbook as sources of information.*

Spanish Netherlands	Bohemia	Prague	Denmark
Sweden	Rome	Geneva	Portugal
England	Amsterdam	Münster	Worms
Paris	English Channel	Antwerp	Russia to 1505
London	Bavaria	Papal States	Moscow
Scotland	Nantes	Wittenberg	Belgrade

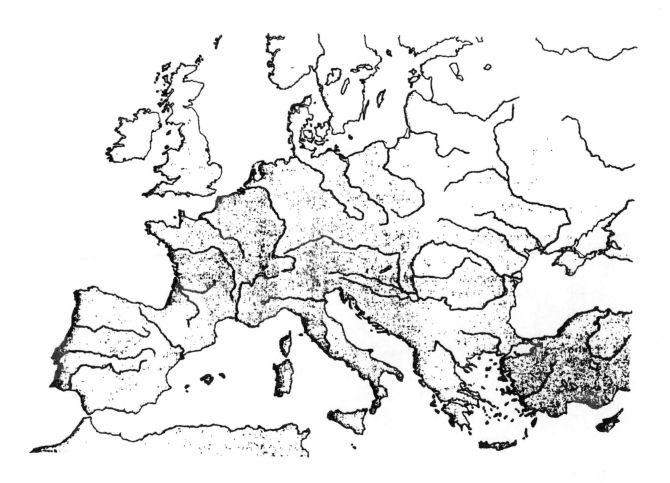

152

ARRIVING AT CONCLUSIONS

Here is a quotation from a historian dealing with the significance of this period of history. Answer the accompanying questions briefly, and be prepared to defend your position.

1. After several years of conflict, the armies of Ferdinand II and the Catholic League gained the upper hand over their Protestant opponents. In 1626, the intervention of the Danish king on behalf of the Protestants was halted, and other Protestant forces were defeated by Wallenstein. These successes, Robert Bireley observes, produced an ambivalent reaction in the Catholic camp.

   "As the Catholic position in the Empire grew stronger, a struggle began to develop within the Catholic camp over the way to exploit their advantage. The more militant spirits discerned in the Catholic triumphs a divine summons to roll Protestantism back still further, as well as a pledge of divine aid. They looked upon any compromise with the Protestants as a pusillanimous lack of confidence in God, and they sometimes referred with disdain to their rivals as *politici*, a term that for them frequently connoted lack of religious principle much as the word "politician," . . . suggests dishonesty today. More moderate figures were inclined toward a peace settlement that would consolidate Catholic gains even at the expense of some concessions to the Protestants. For them, to prolong the war was only to overextend the resources of the Catholics, to imperil the gains already made on behalf of Church and Empire, and to visit still more woe on the long-suffering population." (Robert Bireley, *Religion and Politics in the Age of the Counterreformation* [Chapel Hill: University of North Carolina Press, 1981], p. 23.)

To what extent could the length and the costs of the Thirty Years' War have been predicted in 1626? What advantages did the militants have over the moderates in this debate among Catholic leaders? Would you agree or disagree that the point of view of the militants is like that of many modern, ideologically inspired revolutionary or counterrevolutionary movements?

QUESTIONS TO THINK ABOUT

1. The Hundred Years' War was brought about by a combination of factors that included self-interest, religion, and nationalism. How are wars today similar, and how are they different?

2. It has been said that Spain's decline was due as much to the decay of its domestic economy as to the excessive spending of its resources on war. Explain. Do you think that the United States might find itself in a similar situation?

3. To what extent was the Thirty Years' War a religious conflict? To what extent was it a political and economic struggle?

4. By 1648, to what extent had European nation-states left behind influences of the Middle Ages, and to what extent had they become modern nation-states? Explain your answer.

5. In what ways was state-building in Russia in this period similar to other nations in Europe, and in what ways was it different? Explain your answer, citing specific examples.

CHAPTER 16

Global Encounters: Europe and the New World Economy, 1400–1650

The expansion of European colonial empires into Asia, Africa, and the Americas was a major world event. Before the mid-fifteenth century, Europe was characterized by a growing scarcity of land, making social mobility difficult. There were limited opportunities for individuals to break out of the rigid class structure, which was based on limited land and constricted economic opportunities. There was constant conflict: in England, the Wars of the Roses; in France, religious war; in Spain, the fight to drive out the Muslims; and in eastern Europe, the threat of conquest from Ottoman Turkey. With the advent of European voyages of exploration, the whole atmosphere changed. Governments were forced to think in global terms. Merchant classes now found the means to break medieval fetters and to lay the foundations for capitalism that launched the modern nation-states of today.

The civilizations of the Americas, Africa, India, Southeast Asia, and East Asia were challenged by the global commercial network that produced wealth through exchanges of goods. Some of these civilizations were subsequently conquered; others became marginalized in a world system that judged them undeveloped when faced with the technological change that followed closely on the heels of European empire expansion.

In the course of European expansion, European populations were planted in the Western Hemisphere, and the New World became dominated by European culture while Amerindian cultures were absorbed, pushed back, or died out. In the Americas, people would grow up speaking European languages and living under European institutions. In Africa and Asia, the European colonies did not last, but the movements begun by the Portuguese, Spanish, Dutch, French, and English explorers, colonizers, missionaries, and merchants in the fifteenth through seventeenth centuries still constitute a framework of global interrelationships that all peoples must contend with.

YOU SHOULD HAVE A BASIC UNDERSTANDING OF:

Iberia in its "golden age."

The Portuguese and Africa.

The growth of New Spain.

Iberian systems in the New World.

Northern European expansion.

HAVE YOU MASTERED THE BASIC FACTS?

Fill in each of the following blanks with the correct identification.

Iberian Golden Age; Portuguese in Africa

1. _____, _____, _____:
   Three instruments of technology that helped Iberian navigators become more proficient with maritime skills.

2. _____: Portuguese prince whose devotion to scientific exploration and Portuguese imperial and commercial interests fathered the exploration of the African coast and the first rounding of the Cape of Good Hope.

3. _____: Portuguese explorer who first reached the southern tip of Africa.

4. _____: First European to reach India by sailing around the Cape of Good Hope.

5. _____: Portuguese navigator who, sailing for Spain, discovered a passage through the tip of South America; his ships were the first to circle the globe.

6. _____: Agreement in 1494 between Spain and Portugal for the relocation of the line of demarcation between lands reserved for Spanish and Portuguese exploitation.

7. _____: Portuguese base on the west coast of India from which they aided Hindus and traded with the interior.

8. _____: Chinese city in which Portuguese traders were granted permission to reside in 1554.

9. _____: Portuguese viceroy who opened up East Africa and the Persian Gulf through military action.

10. _____ and _____: Two chief commodities that the Portuguese traded for on the West African coast.

11. _____: Sea captain from Genoa who was influenced by Marco Polo's journals to believe that Japan could be reached by a short westward voyage.

12. _____: Spanish discoverer of the Pacific Ocean.

13. _____: French explorer whose sixteenth-century explorations of the St. Lawrence River gave France a claim to northeastern North America.

14. _____: Explorer whose voyages gave England its claim to North America.

15. _____: Spanish conquistador who led the invasion Mexico.

16. _____: Spanish conquistador whose forces overran the area of South America now called Peru.

Growth of New Spain

17. _____: A land and labor grant entitlement in New Spain.

18. _____: Inflation in Europe was greatly accelerated by large imports of this metal from the Spanish American colonies.

19. _____: The Aztec ruler who lost his empire to the Spanish.

Northern European Expansion

20. _____: Dutch trading company that became the instrument through which Holland supplanted Portugal in the Far East.

21. _____: Wealthy Dutch proprietors in North America who held land tracts.

22. _____: A Florentine mariner who mapped the North American coast and established a French claim.

23. _____: Dutch governor-general who founded the Dutch empire in the East Indies.

24. _____: Founded the city of Quebec for New France.

25. _____: The courageous leader of the English colonists at Jamestown in the early, difficult years of the settlement.

26. _____: Banished from Massachusetts for her preaching, this woman established a settlement in Rhode Island.

27. _____: Sixteenth-century German banking family whose financial policies often had international political repercussions.

28. _____: Seaport in the southern Netherlands that was the center of the wool trade and economic hub of Europe until the end of the sixteenth century.

TRY THESE MULTIPLE-CHOICE QUESTIONS

1. _____ The factors encouraging the Iberian states to undertake extensive voyages of exploration include all of the following EXCEPT (1) overpopulation; (2) desire for material gain; (3) advanced maritime technology; (4) religious enthusiasm; (5) improved technology.

2. _____ "Prester John" was supposed to be (1) a Chinese emperor; (2) an Ethiopian king; (3) a tribal ruler in West Africa; (4) the Ottoman sultan; (5) an English pirate.

3. _____ By the fifteenth century, the Portuguese and Spanish had acquired proficiency in (1) the astrolabe; (2) maneuverable square rigging; (3) the compass; (4) all of the above; (5) none of the above.

4. _____ The desire to circumvent the Muslim middlemen in trade with India encouraged the Portuguese to (1) explore the coast of Africa; (2) send explorers into the interior of Africa; (3) establish settlements in Africa and Asia; (4) all of the above; (5) none of the above.

5. _____ All of the following products came into Europe as a result of the voyages of discovery EXCEPT (1) wheat; (2) peanuts; (3) maize; (4) potatoes; (5) tobacco.

6. _____ Which of the following occurred FIRST? (1) discovery of America by Columbus; (2) discovery of Brazil by Cabral; (3) Bartolomeu Dias's voyage around the southern tip of Africa; (4) Dutch penetration of the East Indies; (5) Magellan's circumnavigation of the globe.

7. _____ Prince Henry of Portugal gave assistance to European exploration by all of the following EXCEPT (1) advances in map making; (2) personal leadership of dangerous expeditions around Africa; (3) the development of better ships; (4) the sponsorship of major expeditions; (5) establishment of a famous observatory.

8. _____ The Dominican friar whose reform efforts helped ease the plight of Indians in Spanish colonies was (1) Las Casas; (2) Prester John; (3) de Soto; (4) Cartier; (5) Cabral.

9. _____ Dutch exploration established posts in all of the following Portuguese-explored areas EXCEPT (1) West Africa; (2) Brazil; (3) East Africa; (4) the East Indies; (5) Azores.

10. _____ Choose the number below that gives the correct generalization about the impact of Spanish colonization in Central and South America. (a) The native Amerindian population increased dramatically. (b) Roman Catholic missionaries argued for the rights of the native peoples before the king of Spain. (c) The introduction of the horse, cattle, and many other products of European material culture brought many changes to indigenous civilizations. (d) Representative assemblies were established in the vice-royalties of Mexico and Peru. (1) a and d; (2) b and c; (3) b, c, and d; (4) a and c; (5) only c.

11. _____ By 1650, the Portuguese had lost control of most of their African possessions EXCEPT for (1) Mali; (2) Angola; (3) Kongo; (4) Ghana; (5) none of the above.

12. _____ A major factor working against both Holland and Portugal in the competition for empire was (1) a lack of initiative by citizens and government; (2) their small size and small population; (3) a backward technology; (4) lack of interest in economic expansion; (5) their strong connections with the Roman Catholic Church.

13. _____ The government of the vice-royalties of Mexico City and Peru was entrusted to (1) Indian chiefs; (2) Spanish colonial clergy; (3) high-born Spanish viceroys and aristocratic lawyers; (4) local councils composed of mestizos; (5) mulattoes and peninsulares.

14. _____ Factors in the economic decline of Spain included all of the following EXCEPT (1) lack of cooperation between church and state; (2) neglect of agriculture; (3) the expulsion of skilled workers for religious reasons; (4) long-term trade imbalances; (5) abandonment of the *encomienda* system.

15. _____ Iberian women in the American colonies (1) were legally subordinated to their husbands; (2) comprised about 10 percent of Spanish colonists; (3) were excluded from contact with males throughout their childhood; (4) could not serve in most professional positions; (5) all of the above.

DO YOU KNOW THE SIGNIFICANCE OF THESE TERMS?

In the space provided, identify each of the following terms and evaluate their importance for world history.

Treaty of Tordesillas

Vasco de Gama

Sebastian Munster

prazo

Prester John

conquistadores

Nahuatl

Malintzin

mestizo

caciques

smallpox

Dutch West India Company

Henry Hudson

Samuel de Champlain

Anne Hutchinson

THE PLACE

A.   *On the map on the following page, draw and label a line showing the route of Magellan in his voyage circumnavigating the globe.*

B.   *Draw and label a line showing the route followed by da Gama in his voyage to India.*

C.   *Draw and label a line giving the route of the first voyage of Columbus in 1492.*

D.   *Draw and label a line to indicate the section of North American coast explored by John Cabot for England.*

E.   *Write in the blanks below the number of the location described and its appropriate place name.*

1.   _____, _____: Strait passed by Magellan at the southernmost point of his voyage.

2.   _____, _____: Vast region explored by Coronado.

3.   _____, _____: Cabral reached this part of South America in 1500.

4.   _____, _____: Balboa saw the Pacific from a mountain on this isthmus in 1513.

5.   _____, _____: In 1608, Samuel de Champlain founded a colony here; it became a major city.

6.   _____, _____: Magellan was killed here during his voyage of circumnavigation.

7.   _____, _____: Pizarro destroyed a great empire with his invasion here in 1531.

8.   _____, _____: Domain of the Aztecs, ruled by Montezuma.

9.   _____, _____: Bartolomeu Dias rounded this cape in 1488.

10.   _____, _____: Area reached by the Vikings around 1000 C.E.

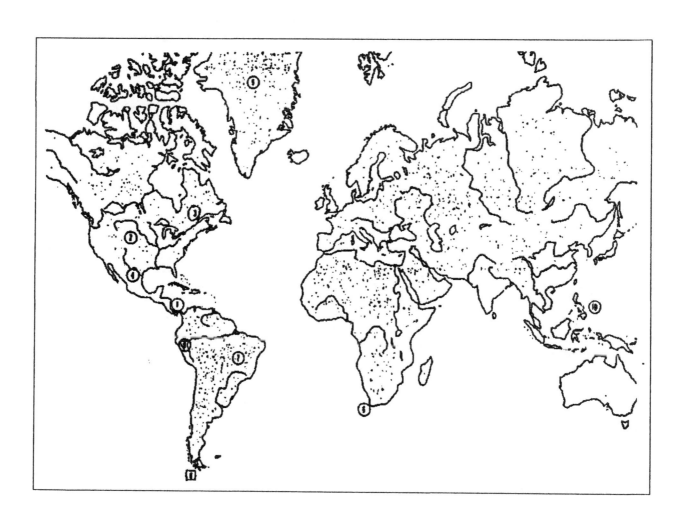

161

RELATIONSHIPS IN TIME

A list of three centuries appears below. Write the names of these explorers under the century in which they made their important contribution, and briefly tell what each one did.

Prince Henry the Navigator
Vasco da Gama
Columbus
Balboa
Magellan

de Soto and Coronado
Cabot
Cartier
Henry Hudson

1400

1500

1600

FOCUSING ON MAJOR TOPICS

Place a T before the statements that are true and place an F before statements that are false..

1. _____ Rising prices of eastern goods made maritime expansion attractive to Spain and Portugal.

2. _____ Through long contact with Muslims at home, the Iberian people had learned to respect the beliefs of non-Christians.

3. _____ The Portuguese directed their explorations southward along the west coast of Africa.

4. _____ The success of Portuguese exploration of the route to India was due in large measure to religious zeal, scientific curiosity, and financial profit.

5. _____ The Portuguese welcomed Columbus's voyage to the Western Hemisphere.

6. _____ By 1550, the Portuguese had gained control of the Indian Ocean from the Muslims.

7. _____ The Spanish conquest of Mexico was made possible by dissension within the Aztec Empire.

8. _____ The Inca Empire was conquered by a large force of Spaniards after meeting stiff resistance.

9. _____ The Spanish organized their conquered territory in the New World into two vice-royalties: Mexico and Peru.

10. _____ The Spanish intermarriage with Indian women produced a mestizo or mixed race.

11. _____ Roman Catholic missionaries argued for the rights of the Amerindians and gave them training in useful crafts.

12. _____ The Spanish monarchs allowed a large measure of self-government in the vice-royalties of Mexico and Peru.

13. _____ The decline of the Amerindian population under Spanish rule was caused by lack of immunity to smallpox and other new diseases carried by the invaders.

14. _____ The large quantities of precious metals that the Spanish took from their colonies in the Western Hemisphere ultimately undermined the Spanish economy.

15. _____ The Spanish government adopted a policy of free trade between its colonies and other European countries.

16. _____ The *encomienda*, the typical pattern of rural society organized by the conquistadors in Mexico, was similar to the manors of medieval Europe.

17. _____ The Portuguese government attempted to suppress the slave trade in its West African possessions.

18. _____ The Swahili states of East Africa lost their independence to the Portugese because they were divided and unused to war.

19. _____ During the seventeenth century, the Dutch drove the Portuguese from all of their African possessions north of Angola.

20. _____ In the Dutch colonial empire, as much effort was made to convert the native population to Christianity as in the Iberian colonial empires.

21. _____ The first wave of English colonists in what is now the state of Massachusetts was composed of religious dissenters called the Pilgrims.

22. _____ Despite initial difficulties, the English established a successful colony at Jamestown in Virginia.

23. _____ English exploration and colonization in the sixteenth and early seventeenth centuries were organized and financed by the central government.

24. _____ Because France was distracted by internal religious conflict and involved in continental wars, it was slow in acquiring a colonial empire.

25. _____ In the early seventeenth century, France established permanent colonies in Canada and in the West Indies.

ARRIVING AT CONCLUSIONS

Here are some quotations from historians dealing with the significance of this period in history. Answer the accompanying questions, and be prepared to defend your position.

1. "Spain did not topple the Indian peoples from an Elysian state of perfection to one of abysmal misery, despite the lyricists who dwell upon the communal happiness of the Incas and the democratic joy of the Aztecs. Spain did not destroy great Indian populations: there never were great populations . . . life was meager and hunger was general before the conquerors came. Spain did not introduce cruelty and war: exploitation was an old story to the Indians. Spain did not destroy human freedom: it had never been enjoyed by Maya, Aztec, [or] Inca. . . . Spain did not destroy ancient systems of noble moral standards. . . . It is possible that the Indians of Mexico and Peru had more to eat under Spanish rule, more protection against each other and against their masters, more security of life and happiness than they had had under Indian nobles and priests. The shift was undoubtedly distasteful, always disruptive, frequently cruel, but it was not a shift from paradise to torment." (Hubert Herring, *A History of Latin America* [New York: Alfred A. Knopf, 1972], pp. 152–53.)

Do you agree with Herring's defense of Spanish colonization? How did Spanish treatment of the Indians compare with that of the British settlers in North America?

2. "The American Indians developed their ways of life in very nearly complete isolation. That isolation not only hampered the growth of their civilizations, but also weakened their defenses against the major diseases of mankind. In the first place, the climate of Siberia, the land bridge and Alaska screened out many diseases; the cold killed the germs and, more important, the cold and the rigor of the life in those latitudes eliminated all humans suffering from debilitating diseases. . . . These first emigrants carried few diseases with them and found no humans in America. . . . They lived, died and bred alone for generation after generation, developing unique cultures and working out tolerances for a limited, native American selection of pathological microlife. When the isolation of the New World was broken, when Columbus brought the two halves of this planet together, the American Indian met for the first time his most hideous enemy: not the white man . . . but the invisible killers which those men brought in their blood and breath." (Alfred W. Crosby, Jr., *The Columbian Exchange: Biological and Cultural Consequences of 1492* [Westport, CN: Greenwood Press, 1975], p. 31.)

How many instances can you think of in which the spread of disease among Amerindians of both North and South America caused them to be unable to challenge the European penetration of the New World? Speculate on the subsequent course of American history if the Aztecs had not been decimated by disease and had defeated Cortez. Would such a defeat have altered the course of Spanish empire building? Would any alteration to Spanish empire building have affected the course of empire building by the other European nations?

3. "Various circumstances are considered to have contributed to the decline of Swahili civilization. There was the Zimba invasion, and it also seems that a decrease in rainfall and the consequent upsetting of the water balance hindered the further development of the coastal towns. . . . However, the chief cause . . . was the disruption of maritime trade by the Portuguese. Being well fitted out, equipped with artillery and built for the purpose of naval warfare, the Portuguese ships were an invincible force. Their constant presence

in the region . . . , the seizure of twenty vessels laden with goods, the defeat of Zanzibar's large fleet of light craft, and the plundering and destruction of the coastal towns . . . were all blows from which East African maritime trade never recovered, and the medieval Swahili civilization perished with it." (V. V. Matveiev, "The Development of Swahili Civilization," in *Africa from the Twelfth to the Sixteenth Century*, ed. D. T. Niane [Berkeley: University of California Press, 1984], pp. 479–80.)

The author stresses the technological and military superiority of the Portuguese. Why did the prosperous and cultivated Swahili city-states fail to recognize that superiority and attempt to match it? Was the force of tradition so strong in African civilizations that it prevented an effective response to European aggression in the early modern period?

QUESTIONS TO THINK ABOUT

1. What factors contributed to the European nations' interest in discovery and exploration in the fifteenth century?

2. How do you account for the continuation of European exploratory activity in the western hemisphere and globally following Columbus's discoveries?

3. Why was the conquest of Amerindian civilizations in the western hemisphere accomplished relatively quickly by the Spanish?

4. Why did European powers not establish any sizeable European colonies in Asia as they did in the Americas?

5. Was discovery by the Europeans a long-term blessing or curse for the Amerindians? Explain.

6. European explorers have been said to have been motivated by "God, gold, and glory." Rank these in the order of importance you feel they played. Be able to defend your judgment by reference to specific individuals.

ANSWER SECTION

CHAPTER 1

BASIC FACTS

1.	hominids	2.	*Homo habilis*	3.	*Homo erectus*
4.	"Eve"	5.	eoliths	6.	Paleolithic
7.	Neolithic	8.	Fertile Crescent	9.	Çatal Hüyük
10.	totem	11.	Stonehenge	12.	Mother Goddess
13.	cuneiform	14.	*Epic of Gilgamesh*	15.	Sargon I
16.	Hammurabi	17.	Pharaoh	18.	monotheism
19.	hieroglyphs	20.	pyramids	21.	Hatshepsut
22.	Osiris cult	23.	Hittites	24.	Phoenicians
25.	Solomon	26.	Abraham	27.	Assyrians
28.	Nebuchadnezzar	29.	Cyrus	30.	Royal Road
31.	Zoroastrianism				

MULTIPLE-CHOICE

1.	(2)	2.	(5)	3.	(5)	4.	(5)	5.	(4)
6.	(1)	7.	(3)	8.	(1)	9.	(3)	10.	(5)
11.	(3)	12.	(3)	13.	(4)	14	(2)	15.	(3)
16.	(2)	17.	(4)	18.	(2)	19.	(2)	20.	(4)
21.	(4)	22.	(4)						

RELATIONSHIPS IN TIME

Paleolithic

use of eoliths
standardization of tools
invention of the bow
first man-made building

Neolithic

Çatal Hüyük
Stonehenge was built
cultivation of grains
use of polished stone tools
domestication of animals
semi-sedentary lifestyle adopted
pyramids of Giza
shift toward food production

CHAPTER 2

BASIC FACTS

1.	Yellow River	2.	Yangzi	3.	Five Sovereigns
4.	oracle bones	5.	Shang	6.	yin, yang
7.	ancestor worship	8.	bronze	9.	Lady Hao
10.	Warring States	11.	*The Book of Documents*	12.	iron
13.	pictographs	14.	Kong Fuzi	15.	*The Analects*
16.	junzi	17.	Mencius	18.	Mandate of Heaven
19.	Zuangzi	20.	Qin	21.	Lord Shang
22.	Shih Huangdi	23.	terra cotta soldiers	24.	Liu Bang
25.	Xiongnu	26.	silk	27.	Wudi
28.	Xu Shen	29.	Liu Xiang	30.	the "Silk Roads"

MULTIPLE-CHOICE

1.	(3)	2.	(4)	3	(3)	4.	(2)	5.	(4)
6.	(2)	7.	(3)	8.	(4)	9.	(5)	10.	(1)
11	(5)	12.	(2)	13.	(1)	14.	(3)	15.	(3)
16.	(3)	17.	(5)	18.	(5)	19.	(4)	20.	(5)

MAKING CONNECTIONS

1.	C	2.	D	3.	M	4.	C	5.	C
6.	L	7	D	8.	M	9.	D	10.	L
11	D	12.	L	13.	M	14.	D	15.	M
16.	M	17.	L	18.	C	19.	D	20.	L

RELATIONSHIPS IN TIME

China

Shang dynasty, 1600–1027 B.C.E.
Zhou dynasty, 1027–221 B.C.E.
Confucius, 551–479 B.C.E.
Qin dynasty, 221–206 B.C.E.
Han dynasty, 206 B.C.–220 C.E.

Fertile Crescent

Old Kingdom in Egypt, 2700–2200 B.C.E.
Hammurabi, 1792–1750 B.C.E.
Moses, 1300 B.C.E.
Assyrian Empire, 745–612 B.C.E.
Persian Empire, 550–331 B.C.E.

CHAPTER 3

BASIC FACTS

1.	India	2.	Indus	3.	Harrapa, Mohenjo Daro
4.	vedas	5.	caste system	6.	Aryans
7.	village, caste, family	8.	Sanskrit	9.	Purusha
10.	reincarnation	11	Untouchables	12.	*brahman*
13.	*Mahabharata*	14.	*Ramayana*	15.	*Upanishads*
16.	Laws of Manu	17.	ahimsa	18.	Mahavira
19.	dharma	20.	Middle Way	21	*Bhagavad-Gita*
22.	*bodhisattvas*	23.	Mahayana	24.	Chandragupta Maurya
25.	Ashoka	26.	*Arthashastra*	27	Gandhara
28.	Bactrian Greeks	29.	Demetrius	30.	Kushanas
31	Deccan	32.	Sangam	33.	monsoons
34.	gold, silver	35.	Lakshmi		

MULTIPLE-CHOICE

1	(3)	2.	(3)	3.	(3)	4.	(5)	5.	(5)
6.	(4)	7.	(5)	8.	(5)	9.	(5)	10.	(2)
11	(2)	12.	(1)	13.	(3)	14.	(4)	15.	(1)
16.	(2)	17.	(4)	18.	(5)	19.	(2)	20.	(3)

MAKING CONNECTIONS

1.	H	2.	B	3.	H	4.	J	5.	B
6.	H	7.	H	8.	H	9.	B	10.	J
11.	B	12.	B	13.	H	14.	B	15.	H

RELATIONSHIPS IN TIME

India

Indus Valley civilization, 2500–1500 B.C.E.
Aryan invasion, 1900–1000 B.C.E.
Later Vedic Age, 1000–600 B.C.E.
Siddhartha Gautama, c. 481 B.C.E.
Mauryan dynasty, 322–185 B.C.E.
Kushan empire, 40 B.C.E.–200 C.E.

Near East and China

Phoenicians, 1000 B.C.E.
King David, 1000–961 B.C.E.
Zoroastrianism, sixth century B.C.E.
Warring States, 475–221 B.C.E.
First Emperor, 221–206 B.C.E.

CHAPTER 4

BASIC FACTS

1.	Minoans	2.	Achaeans	3.	Knossos
4.	Palace of Minos	5.	Mycenae	6.	Arthur Evans
7.	Hisarlik	8.	Linear A	9.	Santorini
10.	Hellen	11.	Persia	12.	Homeric Age
13.	polis	14.	oligarchy	15.	*arete*
16.	Thermopylae	17.	Sparta	18.	laconic farewell
19.	Cleisthenes	20.	Solon	21.	nemesis
22.	Pericles	23.	Peloponnesian War	24.	Herodotus
25.	Thales	26.	Thucydides	27.	Pythagoras
28.	Democritus	29.	Socrates	30.	Plato
31.	Aristotle	32.	Hippocrates	33.	Thespis
34.	Aristophanes	35.	moral virtue	36.	Praxiteles
37.	Hellenistic	38.	Philip II	39.	Alexander the Great
40.	Ptolemy	41.	Epicureanism	42.	Stoicism
43.	Aristarchus	44.	Diogenes	45.	Eratosthenes
46.	Alexandria	47.	Corinthian		

MULTIPLE-CHOICE

1.	(3)	2.	(4)	3.	(1)	4.	(2)	5.	(4)
6.	(3)	7.	(2)	8.	(4)	9.	(1)	10.	(3)
11.	(1)	12.	(3)	13.	(2)	14.	(2)	15.	(4)
16.	(3)	17.	(1)	18.	(4)	19.	(2)	20.	(3)
21.	(2)	22.	(3)	23.	(2)	24.	(5)	25.	(3)

MAKING CONNECTIONS: ATHENS vs. SPARTA

1.	A	2.	A	3.	S	4.	S	5.	A
6.	S	7.	A	8.	S	9.	A	10.	S
11	A	12.	S	13.	S	14.	S		

RELATIONSHIPS IN TIME

Minoan Period: 2000–1450 B.C.E.

Cretan mother goddess
Palace of Knossos

Mycenaean Period: 1450–1200 B.C.E.

Trojan War
Linear B script

Homeric Age: 1150–750 B.C.E.

Iliad and *Odyssey*

Age of Oligarchy: 750–500 B.C.E.

Thales of Miletus
Hesiod's *Works and Days*
Pisistratus
Cleisthenes
Solon
Sappho of Lesbos

Classical Period: 500–336 B.C.E.

Persian Wars
Battle of Marathon
Pericles
Delian League
Peloponnesian War
Philip II conquered the Greek city-states
Socrates
Aeschylus
Sophocles
Euripides
Parthenon
Praxiteles

Hellenistic Age: 336–30 B.C.E.

Alexander the Great
Ptolemaic rulers in Egypt
Seleucid rulers in the Persian Empire
Antigonus the One-Eyed
Skeptics and Cynics
Stoicism
Aristarchus
Greek culture diffused throughout the ancient East and the Roman West

THE PLACE

1	Mycenae	2.	Troy
3.	Italy	4.	Athens
5.	Sparta	6.	Chaeronea
7	Marathon		

CHAPTER 5

BASIC FACTS

1.	Apennines	2.	Romulus, Remus	3.	Etruscans
4.	Latins	5.	Aeneas	6.	*fasces*
7.	Senate	8.	Pyrrhus	9.	Concilium Plebis
10.	Punic Wars	11	Hannibal	12.	Scipio
13.	*pater familias*	14.	Gracchus brothers	15	Julius Caesar
16.	Sulla	17.	*latifundia*	18.	Octavian
19.	Nero	20.	Caligula	21.	*Pax Romana*
22.	Marcus Aurelius	23.	Colosseum	24.	Pompeii or Herculaneum
25.	Essenes	26.	Jesus	27.	St. Paul
28.	martyrs	29.	Constantine	30.	Theodosius
31.	bishop	32.	St. Benedict	33.	St. Augustine
34.	Council of Nicaea	35.	Leo I	36.	Adrianople
37.	Attila	38.	*imperator*	39.	Romulus Augustulus
40.	Theodoric	41	Code of the Twelve Tables	42.	Virgil
43.	Tacitus	44.	aqueduct	45.	Cicero
46.	Stoicism, Epicureanism	47.	Ptolemy	48.	Plutarch
49.	Pantheon	50.	Galen		

MULTIPLE-CHOICE

1.	(1)	2.	(5)	3.	(5)	4.	(1)	5.	(2)
6.	(3)	7.	(4)	8.	(3)	9.	(3)	10.	(2)
11.	(1)	12.	(1)	13.	(2)	14.	(3)	15.	(1)
16.	(3)	17.	(1)	18.	(4)	19.	(2)	20.	(3)
21.	(5)	22.	(1)	23.	(4)	24.	(3)	25.	(3)
26.	(3)	27.	(4)	28.	(2)	29.	(1)	30.	(2)
31.	(4)	32.	(3)						

RELATIONSHIPS IN TIME

A. **The Early Period: Before 509 B.C.E.**

1.	5
2.	4
3.	1
4.	3
5.	2

B. **Early Republic: 509–133 B.C.E.**

1.	4
2.	6
3.	8
4.	1
5.	5
6.	2
7.	7
8.	3

C. **Late Republic: 133–30 B.C.E.**

1.	3, Octavian
2.	1, Sulla
3.	2, Caesar

D. *Pax Romana*: 30 B.C.E.–180 C.E.

1.	3
2.	1
3.	4
4.	2

E. **Christianity, 27–70 C.E.**

1.	5
2.	2
3.	3
4.	4
5.	1

CHAPTER 6

BASIC FACTS

1.	quanats	2.	universalist	3.	Manichaeism
4.	Achaemenid	5.	Ardashir I	6.	Khusraw II
7.	Ctesiphon	8.	caesaropapism	9.	Justinian
10.	Nika rebellion	11	Theodora	12.	Hagia Sophia
13.	themes	14.	Irene	15.	Madaba Mosaic
16.	iconoclastic controversy	17	Mecca	18.	animism
19.	shaykh	20.	Quraysh	21.	Islam
22.	Ka'ba	23.	Allah	24.	Hijra
25.	Hadith	26.	Abu Bakr	27.	Rashiduns
28.	Arabic	29.	Shada ("profession of faith"), Sabat (prayer), Zakat(alms), Sawm (fasting), Hajj(pilgrimage)	30.	Shi'a
31.	Sunni			33.	Muawiya
34.	Damascus	32.	Dome of the Rock		

MULTIPLE-CHOICE

1.	(4)	2.	(2)	3.	(4)	4.	(1)	5.	(5)
6.	(1)	7	(3)	8.	(3)	9.	(3)	10.	(3)
11	(1)	12.	(1)	13.	(5)	14.	(1)		

RELATIONSHIPS IN TIME

A.		B.		C.	
1	3	1	1	1.	5
2.	8	2.	7	2.	7
3.	1	3.	6	3.	1
4.	6	4.	2	4.	3
5.	4	5.	5	5.	9
6.	5	6.	4	6.	6
7.	2	7.	3	7.	8
8.	7	8.	8	8.	4
		9.	9	9.	2

CHAPTER 7

BASIC FACTS

1.	Abu al-Abbas	2.	Baghdad	3.	Harun al-Rashid
4.	vizicr	5.	*amsar*	6.	*ulama*
7.	Shia	8.	Twelfth Imam	9.	Sunni
10.	Sharia	11.	Sufism	12.	jihad
13.	al-Khwarismi	14.	Ibn Sina	15.	Cairo
16.	al-Aziz	17.	Druze	18.	Seljuq Turks
19.	madrasa	20.	Gibraltar	21.	Abd al-Rahman
22.	Abbasid, Fatimid, Umayyad	23.	Reconquista	24.	Crusades
25.	Salah al-Din	26.	Mamluks		

MULTIPLE-CHOICE

1.	(4)	2.	(5)	3.	(3)	4.	(3)	5.	(5)
6.	(1)	7	(2)	8.	(5)	9.	(2)	10.	(2)

RELATIONSHIPS IN TIME

500

600

Muhammad
Hijra
First four caliphs (Rahidun)
Martyrdom of Husayn at Karbala
Muawiya

700

Muslims under Tarik conquer Spain
Umayyads replaced by Abbasids

800

Reign of Harun al-Rahid

900

Rhazes's treatises on medical science

1000

Ibn Sina (Avicenna)
Seljuk Turks capture Baghdad

1100

Ibn Rushd (Averroës)
Salah al-Din

1200

Mongols invade Persia and Iraq
Fall of the Abbasids

1300

1400

Ibn-Khaldun

CHAPTER 8

BASIC FACTS

1	Sahara	2.	savanna	3.	shifting cultivation
4.	*cire perdue*	5.	kinship	6.	Aquatic Age
7	Nok	8.	Meroë	9.	Niger-Congo
10.	Zar'a Ya'kob	11.	Negus	12.	coffee
13.	Ezana	14.	Cathedrals of Roha	15.	*Kebre Negast*
16.	Church of St. Mary of Seyon	17.	Zar'a Ya'kob	18.	Ghana
		20.	Mansa Musa	21.	Askia Muhammad
19.	Islam	23.	Dunama Dibalemi	24.	camels
22.	Timbuktu	26.	Swahili States	27.	Rhapta
25.	Kanem, Bornu, Hausa States	29.	Kilwa	30.	Zheng He
		32.	Great Enclosure	33.	Nyatsimbe Mutota
28.	sultan				
31.	Kongo				

MULTIPLE-CHOICE

1.	(4)	2.	(2)	3.	(3)	4.	(4)	5.	(1)
6.	(3)	7.	(1)	8.	(5)	9.	(5)	10.	(5)
11	(4)	12.	(2)	13.	(4)	14.	(1)	15.	(3)
16.	(2)	17.	(4)	18.	(3)	19.	(3)	20.	(1)

FOCUSING ON MAJOR TOPICS

1.	Bantu	2.	west central	3.	sorghum
4.	millet	5.	Nok	6.	iron
7.	Kush	8.	Meroë	9.	iron
10.	Aksum	11	Zar'a Ya'kob	12.	Adal
13.	Ghana	14.	Mali	15.	Songhai
16.	Sahara	17.	Niger	18.	coast
19.	Muslim	20.	city-states	21.	Swahili
22.	Arabic	23.	Islam		

CHAPTER 9

BASIC FACTS

1	Gregory I, the Great	2.	Donation of Pepin	3.	Ulfilas
4.	Boethius	5.	The *Book of Kells*	6.	Franks
7.	Merovingian	8.	Carolingian	9.	Arianism
10.	Vikings	11	vassal	12.	fief
13.	knight	14.	subinfeudation	15.	demesne
16.	serfs	17	nobility	18.	chivalry
19.	accolade	20.	suzerain	21	demesne
22.	wrestling, drinking	23.	journeymen	24.	"just price"
25.	guild	26.	Franciscans	27.	Innocent III
28.	heresy	29.	Crusades	30	Philip II Augustus
31.	Henry II	32.	Thomas à Becket	33.	Reconquista
34.	Macedonian	35.	Cyrillic	36.	Anna Comnena
37.	Daniel Nevsky	38.	Mongols, Tatars	39.	Vladimir
40.	Varangians, Rus'	41	Kosovo	42.	Romania

MULTIPLE-CHOICE

1.	(4)	2.	(2)	3.	(4)	4.	(3)	5.	(1)
6.	(2)	7.	(2)	8.	(2)	9.	(1)	10.	(3)
11.	(5)	12.	(1)	13.	(2)	14.	(4)	15.	(2)
16.	(2)	17.	(5)	18.	(2)	19.	(1)	20.	(3)
21.	(5)	22.	(2)	23.	(5)	24.	(4)	25.	(4)
26.	(2)								

RELATIONSHIPS IN TIME

Sixth Century

Clovis unites Franks into one kingdom
Boethius writes *The Consolation of Philosophy*
Benedictine Rule becomes basis for monastic life

Seventh Century

Pontificate of Gregory I

Eighth Century

Charles Martel defeats Muslims at Tours
Venerable Bede writes *Ecclesiastical History of the English People*

Ninth Century

Division of the Carolingian Empire
Charlemagne crowned emperor by the Pope
Viking raids and settlement across Europe

Tenth Century

Election of Hugh Capet

Eleventh Century

Pope Urban II proclaims the First Crusade
Papacy of Gregory VII
Norman Conquest

Twelfth Century

Thirteenth Century

Establishment of the Inquisition
Magna Carta

FOCUSING ON MAJOR POINTS

The Feudal System

Feudalism

CHAPTER 10

BASIC FACTS

1	Gupta	2.	Sanskrit	3.	Hinduism
4.	Chola	5.	Ajanta	6.	Muhammed of Ghazni
7.	Kalidasa	8.	Aryabhatta	9.	Harsha
10.	Rajputs	11	Tamerlane	12.	Urdu
13.	sinification	14.	Empress Wu	15.	Pure Land Sect
16.	Xuanzong	17	Wang An-Shih	18.	An Lushan
19.	Neo-Confucianism	20.	Tang	21	block
22.	Genghis Khan	23.	Kublai Khan	24.	Marco Polo
25.	Yuan	26.	Karakorum	27.	Chengdu
28.	Möngke	29.	John of Monte Corvino	30.	Koguryo
31.	yangban	32.	Yamato	33.	Shintō
34.	shoguns	35.	samurai	36.	Heian
37.	*Tale of Genji*	38.	Nara	39.	*The Pillow Book*
40.	The Hōryūji	41	Zen	42.	Kamikaze
43.	Easter Island	44.	Pacific Islands, Australia, New Zealand		

MULTIPLE-CHOICE

1.	(4)	2.	(3)	3.	(4)	4.	(3)	5.	(3)
6.	(3)	7	(3)	8.	(3)	9.	(1)	10.	(2)
11	(3)	12.	(4)	13.	(4)	14.	(2)	15.	(1)
16.	(4)	17.	(2)	18.	(5)	19.	(1)		

CHAPTER 11

BASIC FACTS

1	Bering Strait	2.	Caval	3.	maize
4.	Olmec	5.	Maya	6.	Aztec
7	Inca	8.	formative	9.	Tenochtitlan
10.	calendar, writing system	11.	Montezuma I	12.	Pachacuti
13.	Cahokia	14.	temple-pyramids	15.	Tollan
16.	long count	17.	*pipiltin*	18.	Iroquois
19.	Adena, Hopewell	20.	Anasazi	21.	Aleuts, Inuit

MULTIPLE-CHOICE

1	(3)	2.	(3)	3	(2)	4.	(4)	5.	(2)
6.	(4)	7	(2)	8.	(4)	9.	(1)	10.	(3)
11	(5)	12.	(4)	13.	(1)	14.	(2)	15.	(1)
16.	(2)	17.	(3)	18.	(3)				

FOCUSING ON MAJOR TOPICS

Mayas, Aztecs, Incas
Aztecs, Incas
4th to 10th centuries
Present-day Mexico and Guatemaula
Architecture, sculpture
Religion: based on Nature, human sacrifice; affected all aspects of society

CHAPTER 12

BASIC FACTS

1.	Asia Minor?	2.	Constantinople	3.	Mehmed II
4.	Osman	5.	Tamerlame	6.	Suleiman
7.	*devshirme*	8.	vizier	9.	Topkapi
10.	*dhimmis*	11.	Safi al-Din	12.	Ismail
13.	Safavi	14.	Abbas	15.	Firdawsi
16.	Babur	17.	Taj Mahal	18.	Akbar
19.	*mansabdars*	20.	Aurangzeb	21.	Kabul
22.	Shaibani Khan				

MULTIPLE-CHOICE

1.	(2)	2.	(4)	3.	(3)	4.	(5)	5.	(1)
6.	(2)	7.	(4)	8.	(5)	9.	(1)	10.	(2)
11.	(2)	12.	(3)	13.	(5)	14.	(1)	15.	(3)
16.	(4)	17.	(1)	18.	(2)				

FOCUSING ON MAJOR TOPICS

1.	S	2.	M	3.	O, S, M	4.	S	5.	O
6.	S	7.	O, S, M	8.	M	9.	O	10.	O
11.	O, S, M	12.	O	13.	O, S, M	14.	S		

CHAPTER 13

BASIC FACTS

1	Red Turbans	2.	Ming Hongwu	3.	eunuchs
4.	Yongle	5.	foot binding	6.	concubinage
7.	*Journey to the West*	8.	*All Men Are Brothers*	9.	porcelain
10.	*Yongle Encyclopedia*	11.	Macao	12.	Jesuits
13.	Qin Liangyu	14.	Zheng He	15.	Confucianism
16.	Wang Yangming	17.	Manchu	18.	Chosŏn
19.	han'gul	20.	Rank Lands	21.	tortoise boats
22.	ceramics	23.	King Sejong	24.	daimyō
25.	Himeji Castle	26.	Toyotomi Hideyoshi	27.	Tokugawa Ieyasu
28.	Sekigahara	29.	Noh Nō	30.	Temple of Golden Pavilion, Temple of Silver Pavilion.
31.	Angkor Wat	32.	Thai		
33.	Islam				

MULTIPLE-CHOICE

1.	(2)	2.	(2)	3.	(2)	4.	(5)	5.	(4)
6.	(4)	7.	(2)	8.	(1)	9.	(3)	10.	(2)
11	(3)	12.	(2)	13.	(4)	14.	(2)	15.	(4)
16.	(2)	17.	(4)						

CHAPTER 14

BASIC FACTS

1	Petrarch	2.	Black Death	3.	Boccaccio
4.	humanism	5.	*quattrocento*	6.	Plato, Aristotle
7.	Botticelli	8.	Michelangelo	9.	da Vinci
10.	Mannerism	11.	Erasmus	12.	*Utopia*
13.	Montaigne	14.	Shakespeare	15.	Rabelais
16.	Dürer	17.	Cervantes	18.	van Eyck
19.	Gutenberg	20.	Boniface VIII	21	Hus
22.	Great Schism	23.	Holy Roman Empire	24.	Tetzel
25.	justification by faith	26.	Leo X	27	Charles V
28.	Diet of Worms	29.	Wycliffe	30.	indulgences
31	Ninety-Five Theses	32.	Peace of Augsburg	33.	Henry VIII
34.	Zwingli	35.	Calvin	36.	Anabaptists
37	Queen Mary	38.	Hugenots	39.	Council of Trent
40.	Loyola	41.	Savanarola	42.	St. Teresa of Avila
43.	Pope Paul III				

MULTIPLE-CHOICE

1	(2)	2.	(5)	3.	(5)	4.	(1)	5.	(3)
6.	(5)	7	(4)	8.	(3)	9.	(3)	10.	(5)
11	(1)	12.	(2)	13.	(4)	14.	(3)	15.	(2)
16.	(2)	17	(1)	18.	(2)	19.	(5)	20.	(1)
21	(2)	22.	(1)	23.	(3)	24.	(3)	25.	(2)
26.	(1)	27.	(5)	28.	(2)	29.	(4)	30.	(1)
31	(2)								

FOCUSING ON MAJOR TOPICS

1	S	2.	H	3.	H	4.	S	5.	S
6.	H	7	H	8.	S	9.	H	10.	H
11.	H	12.	H	13.	H	14.	S		

RELATIONSHIPS IN TIME

Italian Renaissance

1300

      Petrarch
      Giotto
      Boccaccio

1400

      Ghiberti
      Donatello
      Medici family ruled Florence
      Brunelleschi

1500

      Botticelli
      Bramante
      Leonardo da Vinci
      Raphael
      Michelangelo

Giorgione
Titian
Josquin des Prés

Northern Renaissance

1400

Gutenberg's Bible
Jan van Eyck

1500

Erasmus
Sir Thomas More
Ulrich von Hutten
Montaigne
Dürer
Holbein the Younger
Brueghel the Elder

1600

Cervantes
Shakespeare

The Protestant Reformation in Germany

1. 2
2. 4
3. 3
4. 1

The Protestant Revolt in England

1. 4
2. 1
3. 3
4. 2

The Catholic Counter-Reformation

1. 3
2. 5
3. 1
4. 2
5. 4

CHAPTER 15

BASIC FACTS

1. long bow
2. Joan of Arc
3. Wars of the Roses
4. Louis XI
5. Inquisition
6. Granada
7. Catholic Majesties
8. Habsburg
9. Golden Bull
10. Hanseatic League
11. *condotierri*
12. Philip II
13. Matthias Corvinus
14. William of Orange
15. Council of Blood
16. Massacre of St. Bartholomew's Eve
17. Mary
18. John Knox
19. Armada
20. Lepanto
21. defenestration of Prague
22. Gustavus Adolphus
23. Simplicissimus
24. Edict of Nantes
25. Treaty of Westphalia
26. Moscow
27. Ivan III
28. Kremlin
29. Paleologus
30. 1453
31. Battle of Kahlenberg

MULTIPLE-CHOICE

1.	(5)	2.	(4)	3.	(2)	4.	(1)	5.	(1)
6.	(4)	7	(3)	8.	(3)	9.	(2)	10.	(1)
11.	(5)	12.	(4)	13.	(5)				

FOCUSING ON MAJOR TOPICS

1.	Habsburgs	2.	Ferdinand	3.	Philip II
4.	Lepanto	5.	William	6.	independence
7.	Elizabeth I	8.	Spanish Armada	9.	1588

CHAPTER 16

BASIC FACTS

1.	compass, astrolabe, lateen sail	2.	Prince Henry	3.	Dias
4.	da Gama	5.	Magellan	6.	Treaty of Tordesillas
7.	Goa	8.	Macao	9.	Albuquerque
10.	slaves, gold	11.	Columbus	12.	Balboa
13.	Cartier	14.	Cabot	15.	Cortez
16.	Pizarro	17.	*encomienda*	18.	silver
19.	Montezuma	20.	Dutch East India Company	21.	patroons
22.	Verazzano	23.	Coen	24.	Champlain
25.	Captain John Smith	26.	Anne Hutchinson	27.	Fuggers
28.	Antwerp				

MULTIPLE-CHOICE

1	(1)	2.	(2)	3.	(4)	4	(1)	5.	(1)
6.	(3)	7	(2)	8.	(1)	9.	(2)	10.	(2)
11.	(2)	12.	(2)	13.	(3)	14.	(1)	15.	(4)

THE PLACE

1	(8)	Strait of Magellan	2.	(2)	American West
3.	(7)	Brazil	4.	(1)	Panama
5.	(3)	Quebec	6.	(10)	Philippines
7.	(9)	Peru	8.	(4)	Mexico
9.	(6)	Cape of Good Hope	10.	(5)	Greenland

RELATIONSHIPS IN TIME

1400	1500	1600
Prince Henry the Navigator	Balboa	Henry Hudson
Vasco da Gama	Magellan	
Columbus	de Soto and Coronado	
Cabot	Cartier	

FOCUSING ON MAJOR TOPICS

1.	T	2.	F	3.	T	4.	T	5.	F
6.	T	7.	T	8.	F	9.	T	10.	T
11.	T	12.	F	13.	T	14.	T	15.	F
16.	T	17.	F	18.	T	19.	T	20.	F
21.	T	22.	T	23.	F	24.	T	25.	T